N

HOLLAND

BELGIUM

LUXEMBOURG

Spangdahlem

Wiesbaden

Rhine River

GERMANY

Marville

Etain.

Phalsbourg

Toul.

Strasbourg

Chaumont

51°

49°

47°

6°

9°

11°

● City   ⬚ Storm Area Forecast

0   25   50   75   100

SCALE OF MILES

STRANGER TO THE GROUND

Books by Richard Bach

JONATHAN LIVINGSTON SEAGULL

BIPLANE

STRANGER TO THE GROUND

STRANGER TO

By *Richard Bach*

Introduction by Gill Robb Wilson

HARPER & ROW, PUBLISHERS

NEW YORK, EVANSTON, SAN FRANCISCO, LONDON

1817

THE GROUND

A portion of this book originally appeared in the July 1963 issue of *Harper's Magazine*.

STANDARD BOOK NUMBER: 06-010180-6

LIBRARY OF CONGRESS CATALOG CARD NUMBER: 63-14370

To Don Slack
And to a mountain in central
France that stands 6,188 feet
above sea level

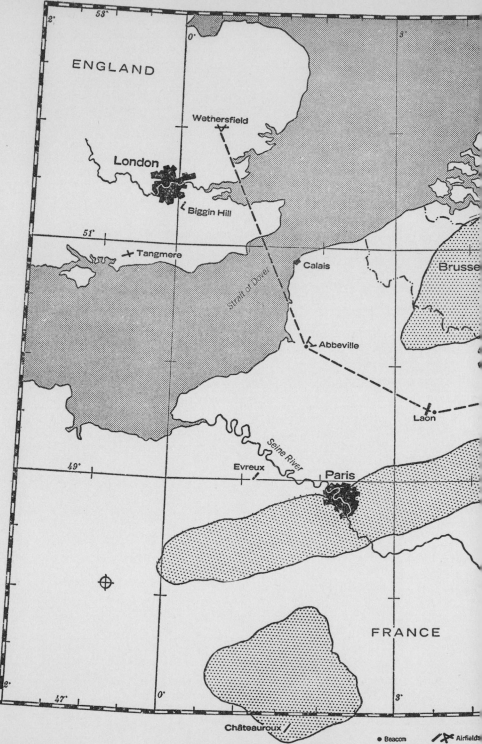

ENGLAND

Wethersfield

London

Biggin Hill

51°

Tangmere

Calais

Brusse

Strait of Dover

Abbeville

Laon

Seine River

49°

Evreux

Paris

2°

53°

0°

3°

FRANCE

2°

47°

0°

3°

Châteauroux

● Beacon

Airfield

Map by Harry Scott

N

HOLLAND

BELGIUM

LUXEMBOURG

Marville

Etain

Toul

Chaumont

Spangdahlem

Phalsbourg

Wiesbaden

Rhine River

GERMANY

Strasbourg

53°   11°

6°

51°

49°

6°   9°   47°   11°

City   Storm Area Forecast

0   25   50   75   100
SCALE OF MILES

Preface to the Second Printing

I could have sworn this book was written a long time ago. Ten years gone, and that is a long time, flying airplanes.

Ten years from the night I stepped at last down the yellow ladder of page 173 to finish a flight and a story. Ten years—returned to the United States and moved a thousand miles from the New Jersey Air National Guard; ten years and joined the Iowa Air Guard and thrown out, grounded and outcast for failing to cut my civilian mustache; ten years and thousands of hours in little airplanes landing free in hidden meadows and tiny airports, careful not to see the silver contrails of those who flew where once I flew. I could have sworn that ten years was a long time.

Nowadays the fighter planes have rafts of electronics, two engines, two pilots and no guns at all; just missiles to fire to keep idle hands from boredom. It sounds today as if the kind of person who lived this book is flown further gone than will ever be seen again.

But you know, maybe not. Yesterday a Navy pilot told the press that he flew because he liked to fly. And today an Air Force aviator said that flying was his life, and if to fly these airplanes one has to fight a war, well that's the way it is. None of them mentioned why, or said just what it is that makes them so like to fly.

And I thought, well what do you think of that. Maybe the old loves, the old reasons why are as true as ever.

Only the faces in the cockpits have changed . . . there are still pilots flying white-starred airplanes in the world and flying red-starred ones, patrolling borders as assigned, yet wondering all the while about the man cruising parallel on the other side.

Whether this is sad is for you to say. But sad or not, there is this very moment a pilot here and one there clinking out to his airplane glad that it exists, be the machine American-made or Soviet, Chinese or Brazilian, Indian or Dutch or British or French. Ten years gone, and still there's many a solemn face and careful concern for exhaust gas temperature and limiting mach and the frail circuits of a UHF radio; many a man reluctant to say why it is that his life would be empty without these things.

A book is never finished. It's always waiting with every new reading to be figured out. It may be that *Stranger*--one pilot's why, as true for his calling as the sailor's why is true for his sea—was not only written just a moment ago, but that it isn't a story about flying at all.

Another moment, another ten years, perhaps, and I'll know.

RICHARD BACH

Bridgehampton, N.Y.
1972

Introduction

Stranger to the Ground, above all else, is an insight into the character of a man whose great compulsion is to measure himself against storm and night and fear.

On the surface it is the tale of a memorable mission of a young fighter pilot utilizing his skills in a lonely duel with death. Yet between the lines emerges the portrait of the airman as a breed, probing outward, but even more significantly, inward.

To be written, this book had first to be flown! Whoever reads it will find himself locked· in a cockpit with Dick Bach, not for a single flight but for a thousand preceding hours in which professional skills were polished to combat competency, and a philosophy of life was matured.

It is rarely realized—and this may be as appropriate a place as any to point it out—that in the achievement of flight men have perhaps had to call more deeply on resources of heart and mind than in any previous reach of experience.

There is nothing in man's physical nature which prepares him for flight. Countless generations have rooted human instincts in earth-bound habits.

Everything pertaining to flight has had to be invented—the aircraft; the instruments; the engines; the guidance systems; the communications; the airports—everything. And beyond this, men have had to meld myriad scientific discoveries into workable compromises, lending themselves in the process to unprecedented experiments.

As I contemplate all this after a lifetime of intimate association with it, I marvel at the depth of man's spiritual and intellectual resources more than at the altitudes and speeds of his flight.

Our modern triumph in reaching toward the stars is as much an extension of the human spirit as it is a breakthrough in science. Science is the servant. Spirit is the master.

This is the message of *Stranger to the Ground,* gleaming through the love of a pilot for his plane, the dedication of an officer to his country, the determination of a young man to pay his debt to freedom in combat with storm and night and fear.

GILL ROBB WILSON

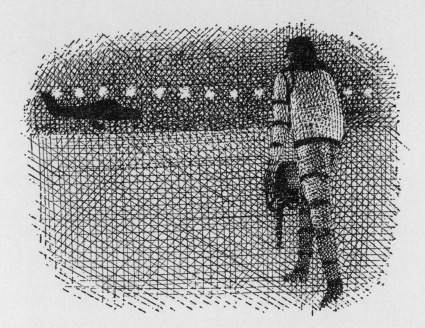

CHAPTER ONE

The wind tonight is from the west, down runway two
eight. It pushes gently at my polka-dot scarf and makes
the steel buckles of my parachute harness tinkle in the
darkness. It is a cold wind, and because of it my takeoff
roll will be shorter than usual and my airplane will climb
more quickly than it usually does when it lifts into the sky.

Two ground crewmen work together to lift a heavy padlocked canvas bag of Top Secret documents into the nose
of the airplane. It sags awkwardly into space normally oc-
cupied by contoured ammunition cans, above four oiled
black machine guns, and forward of the bomb release com-

puters. Tonight I am not a fighter pilot. I am a courier for 39 pounds of paper that is of sudden urgent interest to my wing commander, and though the weather this night over Europe is already freakish and violent, I have been asked to move these pounds of paper from England into the heart of France.

In the bright beam of my flashlight, the Form One, with its inked boxes and penciled initials, tells me that the airplane is ready, that it carries only minor shortcomings of which I already know: a dent in one drop tank, an inspection of the command radio antenna is due, the ATO* system is disconnected. It is hard to turn the thin pages of the Form One with gloves on, but the cold wind helps me turn them.

Form signed, gun bay door locked over the mysterious canvas bag, I climb the narrow yellow ladder to my dark cockpit, like a high-booted mountain climber pulling himself to a peak from whose snows he can stand and look down upon the world. My peak is the small cockpit of a Republic F-84F *Thunderstreak*.

The safety belt of the yellow-handled ejection seat is wide nylon web, heavy and olive-drab; into its explosive buckle fits the nylon harness from over my shoulders and the amber steel link that automatically opens my parachute if I should have to bail out tonight. I surround myself with the universal quiet metallic noises of a pilot joining himself to his airplane. The two straps to the seat cushion survival kit, after their usual struggle, are captured and clink softly to my parachute harness. The green oxygen mask fits into its regulator hose with a muffled rubbery snap. The steel D-ring lanyard clanks as it fastens to the curved bar of the parachute ripcord handle. The red-streamered ejec-

* A glossary of technical terms will be found on page 175.

[2]

tion seat safety pin scrapes out of its hole drilled in the trigger of the right armrest and rustles in the darkness into the small pocket on the leg of my tight-laced G-suit. The elastic leg strap of my scratched aluminum kneeboard cinches around my left thigh, latching itself with a hollow clank. My hard white fiberglass crash helmet, dark-visored, gold-lettered 1/LT. BACH, fits stiffly down to cover my head, its soft sponge-rubber earphones waiting a long cold moment before they begin to warm against my ears. The chamois chinstrap snaps at the left side, microphone cable connects with its own frosty click into the aircraft radio cord, and at last the wind-chilled green rubber oxygen mask snugs over my nose and mouth, fitting with a tight click-click of the smooth chromed fastener at the right side of the helmet. When the little family of noises is still, by tubes and wires and snaps and buckles, my body is attached to the larger, sleeping body of my airplane.

Outside, in the dark moving blanket of cold, a ghostly yellow auxiliary power unit roars into life, controlled by a man in a heavy issue parka who is hoping that I will be quick to start my engine and taxi away. Despite the parka, he is cold. The clatter and roar of the big gasoline engine under his hands settles a bit, and on its voltage dials, white needles spring into their green arcs.

From the engine of the power unit, through the spinning generator, through the black rubber snake into the cold silver wing of my airplane, through the marked wires of the DC electrical system, the power explodes in my dark cockpit as six brilliant red and yellow warning lights, and as quick tremblings of a few instrument pointers.

My leather gloves, stamped with the white wings and star of Air Force property, go through a familiar little act for the interested audience that watches from behind my eyes.

[3]

From left to right around the cockpit they travel; checking left console circuit breakers in, gun heater switch *off*, engine screen switch *extend*, drop tank pressure switches *off*, speed brake switch *extend*, throttle *off*, altimeter, drag chute handle, sight caging lever, radiocompass, TACAN, oxygen, generator, IFF, inverter selector. The gloves dance, the eyes watch. The right glove flourishes into the air at the end of its act and spins a little circle of information to the man waiting in the wind below: checks are finished, engine is starting in two seconds. Now it is throttle on, down with the glove, and starter switch to *start*.

There is no time to take a breath or blink the eye. There is one tiny tenth-second hiss before concussion shatters icy air. Suddenly, instantly, air and sparks and Jet Propellant Four. My airplane is designed to start its engine with an explosion. It can be started in no other way. But the sound is a keg of black powder under the match, a cannon firing, the burst of a hand grenade. The man outside blinks, painfully.

With the blast, as though with suddenly-opened eyes, my airplane is alive. Instantly awake. The thunderclap is gone as quickly as it came, replaced by a quiet rising whine that peaks quickly, very high, and slides back down the scale into nothingness. But before the whine is gone, deep inside the engine, combustion chambers have earned their name. The luminous white pointer of the gage marked *exhaust gas temperature* pivots upward, lifting as thermocouples taste a swirling flood of yellow fire that twists from fourteen stainless steel chambers. The fire spins a turbine. The turbine spins a compressor. The compressor crushes fuel and air for the fire. Weak yellow flames change to businesslike blue torches held in their separate round offices, and the ghostly power unit is needed no more.

Flourish with the right glove, finger pointing away; away the power, I'm on my own.

[4]

Tailpipe temperature is settled and at home with 450 degrees of centigrade, tachometer steadies to note that the engine is turning at 45 percent of its possible rpm. The rush of air to the insatiable steel engine is a constant rasping scream at the oval intake, a chained banshee shrieking in the icy black air and the searing blue fire.

Hydraulic pressure shows on a dial, under a pointer. Speed brake switch to *retract,* and the pressure pulls two great slabs of steel to disappear into the smooth sides of my airplane. Rainbow lights go dark as pressure rises in systems for fuel and oil. I have just been born, with the press of wind at my scarf. With the wind keening along the tall swept silver of my rudder. With the rush of wind to the torches of my engine.

There is one light left on, stubbornly glowing over a placard marked *canopy unlocked.* My left glove moves a steel handle aft. With the right I reach high overhead to grasp the frame of the counterbalanced section of double-walled plexiglass. A gentle pull downward, and the smooth-hinged canopy settles over my little world. I move the handle forward in my left glove, I hear a muffled sound of latches engaging, I see the light wink out. The wind at my scarf is gone.

I am held by my straps and my buckles and my wires in a deep pool of dim red light. In the pool is all that I must know about my airplane and my position and my altitude until I pull the throttle back to *off,* one hour and 29 minutes and 579 airway miles from Wethersfield Air Base, England.

This base means nothing to me. When I landed it was a long runway in the sunset, a tower operator giving taxi directions, a stranger waiting for me in Operations with a heavy padlocked canvas bag. I was in a hurry when I arrived, I am in a hurry to leave. Wethersfield, with its hedges and its oak trees that I assume are part of all English towns, with its stone houses and mossed roofs and its people who watched the Battle of Britain cross the sky with black smoke, is to me Half Way. The sooner I leave Wethersfield a smudge in the darkness behind, the sooner I can finish the letter to my wife and my daughter, the sooner I can settle into a lonely bed and mark another day gone from the calendar. The sooner I can take myself beyond the unknown that is the weather high over Europe.

On the heavy black throttle under my left glove there is a microphone button, and I press it with my thumb. "Wethersfield Tower," I say to the microphone buried in the snug green rubber of my oxygen mask. I hear my own voice in the earphones of my helmet, and know that in the high glass cube of the control tower the same voice and the same words are this moment speaking. "Air Force Jet Two Niner Four Zero Five; taxi information and standing by for ATC clearance."

It still sounds strange. Air Force Jet. Six months ago it was Air Guard Jet. It was one weekend a month, and fly when you have the spare time. It was the game of flying better than Air Force pilots and shooting straighter than Air Force pilots, with old airplanes and with a full-time civilian job. It was watching the clouds of tension mushroom over the world, and knowing for certain that if the country needed more firepower, my squadron would be a part of it. It was thirty-one pilots in the squadron knowing that fact, knowing that they could leave the squadron before the recall came; and it was the same thirty-one pilots, two months later, flying their worn airplanes without inflight refueling, across the Atlantic into France. Air Force Jet.

"Roger, Zero Five," comes a new voice in the earphones.

[6]

"Taxi runway two eight; wind is two seven zero degrees at one five knots, altimeter is two niner niner five, tower time is two one two five, clearance is on request. Type aircraft, please."

I twist the small knurled knob near the altimeter to set 29.95 in a red-lit window. The hands of the altimeter move slightly. My gloved thumb is down again on the microphone button. "Roger, tower, Zero Five is a Fox Eight Four, courier: returning to Chaumont Air Base, France."

Forward goes the thick black throttle and in the quickening roar of startled, very hot thunder, my Republic F-84F, slightly dented, slightly old-fashioned, governed by my left glove, begins to move. A touch of boot on left brake and the airplane turns. Back with the throttle to keep from blasting the man and his power unit with a 600-degree hurricane from the tailpipe. Tactical Air Navigation selector to *transmit and receive*.

The sleeping silver silhouettes of the F-100's of Wethersfield Air Base sweep by in the dark as I taxi, and I am engulfed in comfort. The endless crackle of light static in my earphones, the intimate weight of my helmet, the tremble of my airplane, rocking and slowly pitching as it rolls on hard tires and oil-filled struts over the bumps and ridges of the taxiway. Like an animal. Like a trusted and trusting eager heavy swift animal of prey, the airplane that I control from its birth to its sleep trundles toward the two-mile runway lulled by the murmur of the cold wind.

The filtered voice of the tower operator shatters the serene static in the earphones. "Air Force Jet Two Niner Four Zero Five, clearance received. Ready to copy?"

My pencil springs from flight jacket sleeve to poise itself over the folded flight plan trapped in the jaws of the clipboard on my left leg. "Ready to copy."

[7]

"ATC clears; Air Force Jet Two Niner Four Zero Five to the Chaumont Airport . . ." I mark the words in scrawled shorthand. I have been cleared to fly the route I have planned. ". . . via direct Abbeville, direct Laon, direct Spangdahlem, direct Wiesbaden, direct Strasbourg, direct Chaumont." A route detoured before it begins; planned to avoid the mass of storms and severe weather that the forecaster has marked in red squares across the direct route to my home base. "Climb in radar control to flight level three three zero, contact Anglia control . . ." The clearance comes in through the earphones and out through the sharp point of the pencil; whom to contact and when and on which frequency, one hour and 29 minutes of flying pressed onto a four-inch square of penciled paper bathed in dim red light. I read the shorthand back to the tower operator, and tap the brakes to stop short of the runway.

"Roger, Zero Five, readback is correct. Cleared for take-off; no reported traffic in the local area."

Throttle forward again and the airplane swings into take-off position on runway two eight. The concrete is wide and long. The painted white stripe along its center is held at one end by my nosewheel, at the invisible other end by the tough nylon webbing of the overrun barrier. A twin row of white edge lights converges in the black distance ahead, pointing the way. The throttle moves now, under my left glove, all the way forward; until the radium-caked tachometer needle covers the line marked *100 percent,* until the tailpipe temperature is up by the short red arc on the dial that means 642 degrees centigrade, until each pointer on each dial of the red-soaked instrument panel agrees with what we are to do, until I say to myself, as I say every time, Here we go. I release the brakes.

There is no instant rush of speed, no head forced against

the headrest. I feel only a gentle push at my back. The stripe of the runway unrolls, lazily at first, beneath the nosewheel. Crackling thunder twists and blasts and tumbles behind me, and, slowly, I see the runway lights begin to blur at the side of the concrete and the airspeed needle lifts to cover 50 knots, to cover 80 knots, to cover 120 knots (go-no-go speed checks OK) and between the two white rows of blur I see the barrier waiting in the darkness at the end of the runway and the control stick tilts easily back in my right glove and the airspeed needle is covering 160 knots and the nosewheel lifts from the concrete and the main wheels follow a half-second later and there is nothing in the world but me and an airplane alive and together and the cool wind lifts us to its heart and we are one with the wind and one with the dark sky and the stars ahead and the barrier is a forgotten dwindling blur behind and the wheels swing up to tuck themselves away in my seamless aluminum skin and the airspeed is up to one nine zero and flap lever forward and airspeed two two zero and I am in my element and I am flying. I am flying.

The voice that I hear in the soft earphones is unlike my own. It is the voice of a man concerned only with business; a man speaking while he has yet many things to do. Still it is my thumb down on the microphone button and my words screened through the receiver in the tower. "Wethersfield Tower, Air Force Jet Two Niner Four Zero Five departing on course, leaving your station and frequency."

My airplane climbs easily through the strange clear air over southern England, and my gloves, not content to accept idleness, move across the cockpit and complete the little tasks that have been assigned to them. The needles of my altimeter swing quickly through the 5,000-foot mark, and while my gloves work at the task of retracting the engine screens, pressurizing the drop tanks, loosing the D-ring lanyard from the ripcord, setting the pneumatic compressor into life, I notice suddenly that there is no moon. I had hoped for a moon.

My eyes, at the command of the audience behind them, check once again that all the small-dialed engine instruments have pointers properly under their arcs of green paint on the glass. The right glove, conscientious, pushes the oxygen lever from *100 percent* to *normal,* and sets the four white numbers of the departure control frequency in the four black windows of the command ultra-high frequency transmitter.

The strange voice that is mine speaks to the radar control center guiding my departure. The voice is capable of doing the necessary talking, the gloves are capable of moving throttle and control stick to guide the slanting climb of my airplane into the night. Ahead of me, through the heavy angled glass of the windscreen, through a shrinking wall of clear air, is the weather. I can see that it hugs the ground at first, low and thin, as if uncertain that it is over the land that it has been assigned to cover.

The three white hands of the altimeter swing through 10,000 feet, sending my right glove into another, shorter, series of menial tasks in the cockpit. It dials now the numbers 387 into the pie-slice of window on the radiocompass control panel. In the soft earphones are the faint Morse letters A-B: the Abbeville radiobeacon.

Abbeville. Twenty years ago the Abbeville Boys, flying Messerschmitt 109's with yellow-spiral spinners around their propeller-hub cannon were the best fighter pilots in the German Luftwaffe. Abbeville was the place to go when you were looking for a fight, and a place to avoid when you carried canvas sacks instead of machinegun bullets.

[10]

Abbeville on one side of the Channel, Tangmere and Biggin Hill on the other. Messerschmitt on one side and Spitfire on the other. And a tangle of white contrails and lines of falling black smoke in the crystal air between.

The only distance that lies between me and a yellow-nosed ME-109 is a little bend of the river called time. The wash of waves on the sands of Calais. The hush of wind across chessboard Europe. The spinning of one hourhand. Same air, same sea, same hourhand, same river of time. But the Messerschmitts are gone. And the magnificent Spitfires. Could my airplane tonight carry me not along the river, but across the bend of it, the world would look exactly as it looks tonight. And in this same air before them, in another block of old air, the Breguets and the Latés and One Lonely Ryan, coming in from the west, into the glare of searchlights over Le Bourget. And back across the confluences of the river, a host of Nieuports and Pfalzes and Fokkers and Sopwiths, of Farmans and Bleriots, of Wright Flyers, of Santos-Dumont dirigibles, of Montgolfiers, of hawks circling, circling. As men looked up from the ground. Into the sky just as it is tonight.

The eternal sky, the dreaming man.
The river flows.
The eternal sky, the striving man.
The river flows.
The eternal sky, the conquering man.

Tonight Tangmere and Biggin Hill are quiet lighted rectangles of concrete under the cloud that slips beneath my airplane, and the airport near Abbeville is dark. But there is still the crystal air and it whispers over my canopy and blasts into the gaping oval intake a gun's length ahead of my boots.

It is sad, to be suddenly a living part of what should be-

[11]

long to old memory and faded gun-camera films. My reason for being on the far shore of the Atlantic is to be always ready to mold new memories of the victory of Us against Them, and to squeeze the trigger that adds another few feet to history's reel of gun-camera film. I am here to become a part of a War That Could Be, and this is the only place I belong if it changes into a War That Is.

But rather than learning to hate, or even to be more uncaring about the enemy who threatens on the other side of the mythical iron curtain, I have learned in spite of myself that he might actually be a man, a human being. During my short months in Europe, I have lived with German pilots, with French pilots, Norwegian pilots, with pilots from Canada and from England. I have discovered, almost to my surprise, that Americans are not the only people in the world who fly airplanes for the sheer love of flying them. I have learned that airplane pilots speak the same language and understand the same unspoken words, whatever their country. They face the same headwinds and the same storms. And as the days pass without war, I find myself asking if a pilot, because of the political design under which he lives, can possibly be a totally different man from all the pilots living in all the political systems across the earth.

This man of mystery, this Russian pilot about whose life and thoughts I know so little, becomes in my mind a man not unlike myself, who is flying an airplane fitted with rockets and bombs and machine guns not because he loves destruction but because he loves his airplane, and the job of flying a capable, spirited airplane in any Air Force cannot be divorced from the job of killing when there is a war to be fought.

I am growing to like this probable pilot of the enemy, the

more so because he is an unknown and forbidden man, with no one to bear witness of the good in him, and so many at hand to condemn his evils.

If war is declared here in Europe, I will never know the truth of the man who mounts the cockpit of a red-starred airplane. If war is declared, we are unleashed against each other, like starved wolves, to fight. A friend of mine, a true proven friend, neither imagined nor conjured out of possibilities, will fall to the guns of a Russian pilot. Somewhere an American will die under his bombs. In that instant I will be swallowed up in one of the thousand evils of war; I will have lost the host of unmet friends who are the Russian pilots. I will rejoice in their death, take pride in the destruction of their beautiful airplanes under my own rockets and my own guns. If I succumb to hate, I will myself become certainly and unavoidably a lesser man. In my pride I will be less worthy of pride. I will kill the enemy, and in so doing will bring my own death upon me. And I am sad.

But this night no war has been declared. It seems, in the quiet days, almost as if our nations might learn to live with each other, and this night the eastern pilot of my imagining, more real than the specter he would become in wartime, is flying his own solitary airplane into his own capricious weather.

My gloves are at work again, leveling the airplane at 33,000 feet. Throttle comes back under the left glove until the engine tachometer shows 94 percent rpm. The thumb of the right glove touches the trim button on the control stick once and again, quickly, forward. The eyes flick from instrument to instrument, and all is in order. Fuel flow is 2,500 pounds per hour. Mach needle is resting over .8, which means that my true airspeed is settling at 465 knots. The thin luminous needle of the radiocompass, over its many-numbered dial, pivots suddenly as the Abbeville radiobeacon passes beneath my airplane, under the black cloud. Eyes make a quick check of transmitter frequency, voice is ready with a position report to air traffic control, left thumb is down on the microphone button at 2200 hours, and the audience behind the eyes sees the first faint flash of lightning in the high opaque darkness ahead.

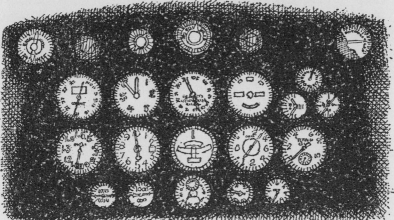

CHAPTER TWO

"France Control, Air Force Jet Two Niner Four Zero
Five, Abbeville." Empty static for a moment in the soft
earphones, and I see, very clearly, a man in a large square
room cluttered with teletypes and speakers and frequency
dials and round grey radar screens. At an upholstered
swivel chair, the man leans forward to his microphone,
setting aside a glass of red wine.

"Four Zero Five, France Control, go ahead." The accent
in his English is barely noticeable. That is rare. He reaches
for a pencil, from a jar bristling with pencils.

The microphone button is down again under my left
thumb, and I hear again the sidetone, just as the man on
the ground is hearing it. The engine in the sidetone is a
quiet and businesslike roar, a waterfall of purposeful sound

that is a background for my message. My words are filtered through the tubed body of the transmitter to become impersonal and faraway, the voice of someone I know only as a casual acquaintance. "France Control, Zero Five is over Alpha Bravo on the hour, flight level three three zero assigned instrument flight rules, estimating Lima Charlie at zero niner, Spangdahlem." Good old France. The only country in Europe where you never say the name of a reporting point, but only its initials, with a little air of mystery as you do. The familiar pattern of the position report is rhythmic and poetic; it is a pattern of pure efficiency that is beautiful to speak. There are thousands of position reports spoken and heard every hour across the earth; they are as basic a part of instrument flying as the calls for landing information are a basic part of fair-weather flight. Position reports are part of a way of life.

"Roger, Zero Five, on your position. Report Lima Charlie." The pencil stops, the wine is lifted.

With his last word, the man at France Control has ceased to exist. I am left alone again with the night and the stars and the sounds of my airplane.

In every other fighter airplane, cruise is a time of quiet and of smooth unvarying sound. The pilot hushes along on his tamed fall of sound and knows that all is well with his engine and his airplane. But not with this airplane, not with my F-84F. My airplane is a clown. Its engine sounds more like a poorly-tuned, poorly-muffled V-8 than a smoothly efficient dynamo spinning on pressure-oiled bearings. I was warned when I began to fly the *Thunderstreak* that if the engine ever stopped vibrating I would be in trouble. It is true. Strange sounds come from nowhere, linger for a while in the body of the airplane, then die away.

Now, behind my left shoulder, a low whine begins. Intrigued by the new tone that my harlequin airplane has discovered, I listen attentively. The whine rises higher and higher, as if a tiny turbine was accelerating to tremendous speed. My left glove inches the throttle back an inch and the whine calms a fraction; throttle forward and it regains its spinning song. In another airplane the whine would be cause for serious and concerned interest; in my airplane it is cause for a slight smile under the green rubber oxygen mask. I had once thought that I had heard all the noises that it was possible for this airplane to make. After a moment, the whine dies away by itself.

Thud. There is the smallest tremor in the throttle, and a sound as if a hard snowball had hit the side of the fuselage. In an F-100 or an F-104, in the new airplanes, the thud would bring a sudden stiffening of pilot and a quick recheck of the engine instruments. In another airplane the thud would likely mean that the engine has thrown a turbine blade, and that a host of unpleasant consequences are to follow. In my '84 though, a thud is just one more sound in the kaleidoscope of sounds that the airplane offers to its pilot, another evidence of an unconforming personality hidden in the metal.

My airplane has a great variety of individual quirks; so many that before we arrived in France it was necessary to arrange a little meeting with the control tower operators, to tell them about the airplane. The boom of the engine start could send the uninitiated scrambling for the fire alarm. When the engine is idling on the ground, turning a modest 46 percent of her available rpm, she hums. She hums not quietly to herself, but an amplified, penetrating, resonant distracting "MMMM" that makes the crew chiefs point painfully to their ears, reminding pilots to advance the power, to increase the rpm past the point of resonance.

It is a very precise and human hum she makes, and there is no doubt over all the airbase that an F-84F is preparing to fly. Heard from a comfortable distance, the airplane is setting the note for the song of her higher thunder. Later, in the sky, there is usually no trace of her resonance, though the cockpit is filled with the other sounds of her engine.

Every once in a while, though, I fly an airplane that hums in the air, and the cockpit is a finely engineered box of torture. Back on the throttle after takeoff, to cruise cross-country, to stay on a leader's wing. MMM . . . Back a little more on the throttle. MMM . . . The resonance ripples through me as if I were a metal servomotor bolted to the fuselage. I shake my head quickly. It is like trying to disperse a horde of hungry mosquitoes with a toss of the head. I open my eyes wide, close them, shake my head again. Futilely. Soon it is difficult to think of flying formation, of cruising, of navigation, of anything but the all-pervading hum that makes the airplane tremble as with a strange malady. Speed brakes out, halfway. Throttle open to 98 percent rpm. The hum subsides with the increased power, replaced by the tremble of air blasting against the speed brakes. To fly two hours in a badly humming airplane would reduce its pilot to a hollow-eyed automaton. I would not have believed that such a simple thing as sound and vibration could erode a man so quickly. When I wrote one airplane up for severe engine resonance, I discovered that it was most often caused by a loose tailpipe connection, allowing the eight-foot tube of stainless steel to rest lightly against the airframe like a tuning fork against a water glass. The perfect tool of a saboteur in wartime would be a wrench with which to loosen, ever so slightly, the tailpipe mounting bolts on enemy airplanes.

Other things. The airplane has a hundred little jokes to

play. A hundred little things that seem to indicate that Something Is Wrong, when nothing at all is amiss. Just before takeoff, during the engine runup on the runway, grey smoke floods into the cockpit, geysering from the air vents. Engine fire? A broken oil line in the engine compartment? No. The cockpit air temperature control is set too cold, and the moist outside air is turned to instant fog by the obedient cooling system. Press the temperature control to *hot* for a moment, and the smoke disappears. And the airplane chuckles to herself.

The same moment, runup. Smoke, real oil smoke, streams from the fuselage, blasting down from a hidden orifice onto the runway, splashing up to wreathe the airplane in grey. Normal. Just the normal oil-mist from the pressure-lubricated bearings, venting overboard as designed.

In flight, after an hour of low-level. Fuel suddenly streams from the leader's airplane, flying back like a great white banner of distress. Broken fuel lines? An indicator of turbine blades spinning from the redhot wheel and an engine coming to pieces? Imminent fire and a burst of scarlet in the sky? No. Quite normal, this streamer of fuel. As the drop tanks feed the last of their fuel, and as the internal tanks join to feed their own fuel, there is for a moment too much JP-4 in the main fuel tank, and it overflows, as designed, harmlessly overboard. The airplane chuckles with an old joke.

Takeoff. Heavy laden at low airspeed, close to the ground, bailout a marginal thing before the flaps are up, and a brilliant yellow light flares on the instrument panel. Suddenly. I see it from the corner of my eye, and I am stunned. For a half-second. And the yellow light, all by itself, goes out. Not the yellow overheat-warning light I saw at that critical moment when fire could be disaster, but the mechanical advantage shift light, telling me, when I have recovered my composure, that the stabilator hydraulic system is going about its task as its destiny demands, changing the response of the flight controls as the landing gear locks up. And the airplane chuckles.

But once in a very long while the turbine buckets do break free and slice redhot through the fuel lines, the fire warning light really does come on with flame at its sensors, the cockpit does fill with smoke. Once in a while. And an airplane screams.

Tonight I cruise. The steady play of whines and thuds and rumbles and squeals, and through it all the luminous needles at 95 percent rpm and 540 degrees tailpipe temperature, and 265 knots indicated airspeed. Cruise is the long radium hands of the altimeter drifting slowly back and forth across the 33,000-foot mark and other shorter needles captured by arcs of green paint on their glass dials. There are 24 round dials on the panel in front of me in the red light. The fact is empty and unimpressive, although I feel, vaguely, as if it should be startling. Perhaps if I counted the switches and handles and selectors . . .

At one time I would have been impressed by the 24 dials, but tonight they are few and I know them well. There is a circular computer on the clipboard strapped to my leg that tells me the indicated airspeed of 265 knots is actually moving my airplane over the land between Abbeville and Laon at a speed of 465 knots, 535 miles per hour. Which is not really fast, but for an old Guard airplane it is not really slow, either.

Cruise. Hours neatly shortened and diced into sections of time spent flying between city and city, radiobeacon and radiobeacon, between one swing of the radiocompass needle and the next. I carry my world with me as I fly, and outside is the familiar, indifferent Other World of fifty-five below zero and stars and black cloud and a long fall to the hills.

From the light static in the earphones comes a quick and hurried voice: "Evreux Tower radio check Guard channel; one-two-three-four-five-four-three-two-one Evreux Tower out."

There is someone else in the world at this moment. There is a tower operator six miles below me, dwindling at 465 knots, who is this second setting his microphone back in its cradle, glancing at his runway held in a net of dim white lights and surrounded by blue taxiway lights that lead to a parking ramp. From his tower he can look down on the tall rhythmic triangles that are the vertical stabilizers of his base's transport airplanes parked. At this moment he is beginning a lonely stretch of duty; his radio check was as much to break the silence as it was to check the emergency transmitter. But now he is assured that the radio works and he settles down to wait the night through. He is not aware that I have passed over his head. To know, he would have to step out to the catwalk around his tower and listen carefully and look up through the last hole in the clouds, toward the stars. He would hear, if his night was a quiet one, the tiny dim thunder of the engine that carries me and my airplane through the sky. If he carried his binoculars, and if he watched at precisely the right moment, he would see the flashing dots of red and green and amber that are my navigation lights, and the white of my fuselage light. And he would walk back into his tower in the first drops of rain and wait for the coming of the dawn.

I remember that I wondered, once, what flying a fighter airplane would feel like. And now I know. It feels just the same as it feels to drive an automobile along the roads of France. Just the same. Take a small passenger sedan to 33,000 feet. Close the walls around the driver's seat, cut away the roof and cap the space with plexiglass. Steer with a control stick and rudder pedals instead of with a wheel. Put 24 gages on the instrument panel. Wear a sage-green set of many-pocketed coveralls and a tight-laced zippered G-suit and a white crash helmet with a dark plexiglass visor and a soft green rubber oxygen mask and a pair of high-topped black jump boots with white shroud-line laces and a pistol in a leather shoulder holster and a heavy green flight jacket with a place for four pencils on the left sleeve and sew your squadron emblem and your name on the jacket and paint your name on the helmet and slip into a parachute and connect the survival kit and the oxygen and the microphone and the automatic parachute lanyard and strap yourself with shoulder harness and safety belt into a seat with yellow handles and a trigger and fly along above the hills to cover eight miles a minute and look down at the growing wall of cloud at your right and watch the needles and pointers that tell you where you are, how high you are and how fast you are moving. Flying a fighter airplane is just the same as driving an automobile along the roads of France.

My airplane and I have been in the air now for 31 minutes since we left the runway at Wethersfield Air Base. We have been together for 415 flying hours since we first met in the Air National Guard. Fighter pilots are not in the cockpits of their airplanes a tenth as long as transport pilots are on the flight decks of theirs. Flights in single-engine airplanes rarely last longer than two hours, and new airplanes replace old models every three or four years, even in the Guard. But the '84 and I have flown together for a reasonably long time, as fighter pilots and their airplanes go. We have gotten to know each other. My airplane comes alive under my gloved touch, and in return for her life she gives me the response and performance that is her love.

I want to fly high, above the cloud, and she willingly draws her own streamer of tunneled and twisting grey behind us. From the ground the tunnel of grey is a contrail of brilliant white, and the world can see, in the slash across the blue, that we are flying very high.

I want to fly low. In a roar, flash, a sweptwing blur we streak across the wooded valleys. We rustle the treetops in the pressure of our passing and the world is a sheetblur in the windscreen with one point fixed: straight ahead, the horizon.

We enjoy our life together.

Every once in a while as an idle hour catches me thinking of the life I lead, I ask why the passion for speed and for low-level flying. For, as an old instructor told me, you can do anything you want in an airplane without the slightest danger, until you try to do it near the ground. It is the contact with the ground, with that depressingly solid other world, that kills pilots. So why do we fly low and fast occasionally just for the fun of it? Why the barrel rolls off the deck after a pass on the army tanks in the war games? Why the magnetism of the bridge, the silent patient dare that every bridge makes to every pilot, challenging him to fly beneath it and come away alive?

I enjoy the color and the taste of life a very great deal. Although death is an interesting sort of thing on the path ahead, I am content to let it find me where it will rather than hasting to meet it or deliberately searching it out. So I ask myself, why the rolls, the lower-than-necessary passes at high speed? Because it is fun, the answer says, throwing up a screen that it hopes will be accepted as self-sufficient. Because it is fun. There. No pilot will deny that. But like a child experimenting with words, I ask, why is it fun? Because you like to show off. Aha. The answer begins to be seen, slipping into a doorway a half-second too late to escape my attention. And why do I like to show off? The answer is caught in a crossfire of brilliant spotlights. Because I am free. Because my spirit is not shackled by a 180-pound body. Because I have powers, when I am with my airplane, that only the gods have. Because I do not have to read about 500 knots or see it in a motion picture from a drone airplane or imagine what it would feel like. In my freedom I can *live* 500 knots—the blur of the trees the brief flash of the tank beneath me the feel of the stick in my right hand and the throttle in my left the smell of green rubber and cold oxygen the filtered voice from the forward air controller, "Nice show, Checkmate!" Because I can tell the men on the ground that truth that I discovered a long time ago: Man is not confined to walk the earth and be subject to its codes. Man is a free creature, with dominion over his surroundings, over the proud earth that was master for so long. And this freedom is so intense that it brings a smile that will not cede its place to mature, dignified impassiveness. For, as the answer said in part, freedom is fun.

She is responsive, my airplane. She does not care that she drinks fuel at low level as a fall drinks water. She does not care that the insects of the forest are snapped into sudden flecks of eternity on her windscreen. She flies at the tops of the trees because that is where I want to fly, because she is a sensitive and responsive airplane. Because I have moved a gloved hand to give her life. Because I paint her a name on the forward fuselage. Because I call her "she." Because I love her.

My love for this airplane is not born of beauty, for a *Thunderstreak* is not a beautiful airplane. My love is born of a respect for quality of performance. My airplane, in the life that I bring to her, expects that I fly her properly and well. She will forgive me the moments that make it necessary to force her where she would not smoothly go, if there are reasons for the moments. But if I continually force her to fly as she was not meant to fly, overspeed and overtemperature, with sudden bursts of throttle, with hard instant changes of flight controls, she will one day, coldly and dispassionately, kill me.

I respect her, and she in turn respects me. Yet I have never said, "We landed" or "We tore the target to pieces"; it is always "I landed," "I knocked out that tank." Without my airplane I am nothing, yet I claim the credit. What I say, though, is not egocentric at all.

I step into the cockpit of my airplane. With shoulder harness and wide safety belt I strap myself to my airplane (I strap on my wings and my speed and my power) I snap the oxygen hose to my mask (I can breathe at altitudes where the air is very thin) I fit the radio cable to the black wire that comes from the back of my fitted helmet (I can hear frequencies that are unheard by others; I can speak to scores of isolated people with special duties) I flick the gun switch to *guns* (I can cut a six-ton truck in half with a squeeze of my finger I can flip a 30-ton tank on its back with the faint pressure of my thumb on the rocket button) I rest one hand on the throttle, one on the contoured, button-studded grip of the control stick (I can fly).

The swept aluminum wings are my wings, the hard

black wheels are my wheels that I feel beneath me, the fuel in the tanks is my fuel which I drink and through which I live. I am no longer man, I am man/airplane; my airplane is no longer merely Republic F-84F *Thunderstreak,* but airplane/man. The two are one, the one is the "I" that stops the tank holding the infantry in its foxholes, that strikes the enemy man/airplane out of the blind sky. The I that carries the wing commander's documents from England to France.

Sometimes I stand on the ground or lie back on a soft couch and wonder how it is possible for me to become wide awake and a part of an airplane, to climb into that fantastically complex cockpit and go through all the procedures and do all the alert thinking that is necessary to fly in formation with other airplanes or around a gunnery pattern for score or to put a cluster of rockets on a target. This thought has stuck with me for long minutes, while I zip the legs of my G-suit, while I slide into my mae west, while I strap myself into the little cockpit. It is a dull lethargy that says, "How can I do everything right?" and wants only to withdraw into itself and forget about the responsibility of flying a high-performance airplane through a precise pattern. But one of the strange features of the game is that as soon as my finger presses the starter switch to *start,* the lethargy vanishes. In that moment I am ready for whatever the mission will require. I am alert and thinking about what has to be done and knowing just how it must be done and taking the flight one step at a time and taking each step surely and correctly and firmly. The feeling of trying to accomplish the impossible disappears with the touch of the switch to my glove and does not reappear until I am again off guard and un-alert and resting before the next flight. I wonder if this is common, this draining of aggressiveness before a flight. I have never asked another pilot about it, I have never heard another pilot speak of it. But as long as the touch of the switch is an instant cure, I am not concerned.

Switch pressed, in the airplane, I asked how I ever found the thought that flying single-engine airplanes is a complicated job. I cannot answer. It just seemed as if that should be, before I start the engine, and long ago, before I understood the 24 dials and the switches and the handles and the selectors. After I sit in one little space for 415 hours I come to know it rather well, and what I don't know about it at the end of that time is not of great importance. Where did the thought of complication begin?

At the air shows, friends who do not fly climb the yellow ladder to my airplane and say, "How complicated it all is!" Do they really mean what they are saying? A good question. I think back, before the day I knew an aileron from a stabilator. Did I once consider airplanes complicated? I think back. A shocking answer. Terribly complicated. Even after I had begun to fly, each new airplane, each larger airplane, looked more complicated than the one I flew before. But a simple thing like knowing the purpose of everything in a cockpit dissolves the word "complicated" and makes it sound foreign when someone uses it to describe my airplane.

This dim red panel in front of me now, what is complex about it? Or the consoles at the left and right? Or the buttons on the stick grip? Child's play.

It was a shattering disillusion, the day I landed from my first flight in the F-84. The *Thunderstreak* was considered then the best airplane in the Air Force for air-to-ground warfare. It could deliver more high explosive on target than any other tactical fighter airplane flying. I was hurt and disillusioned, because I had just gone through fifteen months of marching and studying and flying and Hit One, Mister, to prepare for an airplane that my wife could walk out to and fly any day of the week. I could settle her in the cockpit, put the harness over her shoulders and buckle the seat belt about her and tell her that the throttle is for fast and slow, the stick is for up and down and left and right, and there's the handle that brings the wheels up and down. Oh, and by the way, sweetheart, a hundred and sixty knots down final approach.

There goes the feeling that some magic day I would wake to find myself a superman. My wife, who had spent the last fifteen months taking letters in shorthand, could step into that little cockpit and take it through the speed of sound; could drop, if she wanted, an atomic bomb.

Divorced from my airplane I am an ordinary man, and a useless one—a trainer without a horse, a sculptor without marble, a priest without a god. Without an airplane I am a lonely consumer of hamburgers, the fellow in line at a cash register, shopping cart laden with oranges and cereal and quarts of milk. A brown-haired fellow who is struggling against pitiless odds to master the guitar.

But as "The Speckled Roan" falls to the persistence of an inner man striving with chords of E and A minor and B7, so I become more than ordinary when the inner man strives with the material that he loves, which, for me, has a wing-span of 37 feet 6 inches, a height of 13 feet 7 inches. The trainer, the sculptor, the priest and I. We all share a preference for string beans, and distaste for creamed corn. But in each one of us, as in each of all humanity, lives the inner man, who lives only for the spirit of his work.

I am not a superman, but flying is still an interesting way to make a living, and I bury the thought of changing into a steel butterfly and stay the same mortal I have always been.

There is no doubt that the pilots portrayed in the motion pictures are supermen. It is the camera that makes them. On a screen, in a camera's eye, one sees from without the airplane, looking into the cockpit from over the gunports in the nose. There, the roar of the guns fills the echoing theater and the sparkling orange flames from the guns are three feet long and the pilot is fearless and intense with handsome narrowed eyes. He flies with visor up, so one can see his eyes in the sunlight.

It is this view that makes the superman, the daring airman, the hero, the fearless defender of the nation. From the other side, from alone inside the cockpit, it is a different picture. No one is watching, no one is listening, and a pilot flies in the sun with his visor down.

I do not see gunports or orange flames. I squeeze the red trigger on the stick grip and hold the white dot of the gunsight on the target and I hear a distant sort of pop-pop-pop and smell gunpowder in my oxygen mask. I certainly do not feel like a very daring airman, for this is my job and I do it in the best way that I can, in the way that hundreds of other tactical fighter pilots are doing it every day. My airplane is not a roaring silver flash across the screen, it is still and unmoving about me while the ground does the blurring and the engine-roar is a vibrating constant behind my seat.

I am not doing anything out of the ordinary. Everyone in a theater audience understands that this gage shows how much utility hydraulic pressure the engine-driven pumps are producing; they know perfectly well that this knob selects the number of the rocket that will fire when I press the button on top of the stick grip; that the second button on the grip is a radar roger button and that it is disconnected

[29]

because it is never used; that the button that drops the external fuel tanks has a tall guard around it because too many pilots were pressing it by mistake. The audience knows all this. Yet it is still interesting to watch the airplanes in the motion pictures.

The ease of flying is a thing that is never mentioned in the motion pictures or on the recruiting posters. Flying a high-performance military airplane is exacting and difficult, men, but maybe, if you take our training, you will become a different person, with supernatural power to guide the metal monster in the sky. Give it a try, men, your country needs fine-honed men of steel.

Perhaps that is the best approach. Perhaps if the recruiting posters said, "Anyone walking down this street, from that ten-year-old with his schoolbooks to that little old grandmother in the black cotton dress, is able to fly an F-84F jet fighter airplane," they wouldn't attract exactly the kind of initiate that looks best on a recruiting poster. But just for fun, the Air Force should train a ten-year-old and a grandmother to fly quick aileron rolls over airshows to prove that the tactical fighter pilot is not necessarily the mechanical man that he is so often painted.

There is little to do. I have another six minutes before the wide needle of the TACAN will swing on its card to say that the little French city of Laon has been pulled by beneath me. I drag my tiny cone of thunder behind me for the benefit of the hills and the cows and perhaps a lonely peasant on a lonely walk through the cloudy night.

A flight like tonight's is rare. Normally, when I fit myself into the cockpit of this airplane, there is much to be done, for my job is one of being continually ready to fight. Each day of the week, regardless of weather or holidays or flying schedule, one small group of pilots wakes earlier than all the others. They are the Alert pilots. They awaken and they report to the flight line well before the hour that is Target Sunrise. And each day of each week a small group of airplanes are set aside to wait on the Alert pad, power units waiting by their wing. The airplanes, of course, are armed for war.

After the innocuous flying of the Air National Guard, it is chilling at first to spend the dawn checking the attachment of thousands of pounds of olive-drab explosive under my wings. The Alert procedure sometimes seems an impossible game. But the explosive is real.

The day wears on. We spend an hour studying the target that we already know very well. The landmarks about it, the conical hill, the mine in the hillside, the junction of highway and railroad, are as familiar to us as the hundred-arch viaduct that leads to Chaumont. We have in our minds, as well as on the maps stamped SECRET, the times and distances and headings to the target, and the altitudes we will fly. We know that our target will be as well-defended as anyone's, that there will be a massive wall of flak to penetrate and the delicate deadly fingers of missiles to avoid. Oddly enough, the flak does not really bother us. It does not make a bit of difference whether the target is defended from every housetop or not at all . . . if it is necessary to strike it, we shall go along our memorized route and strike it. If we are caught by the screen of fire, it will be one of those unfortunate happenings of war.

The siren blows, like a rough hand jerking sleep away. My room is dark. For more than a second, in the quick ebb of sleep, I know that I must hurry, but I cannot think of where I must go. Then the second is past and my mind is clear.

The Alert siren.

Hurry.

Into the flight suit, into the zippered black jump boots, into the winter flying jacket. A hurried toss of scarf about throat, leave the door swinging closed and open again on my tousled room and join the rush of other Alert pilots in a dash down the wooden stairs and into the waiting Alert truck. The square wooden buildings of Chaumont Air Base are not yet even silhouettes against the east.

There is a husky comment in the darkness of the rattling truck: "Sleep well, America, your National Guard is awake tonight."

The truck takes us to the airplanes that wait in the dark. The maintenance Alert crew has beaten us to the airplanes, and the APU's are roaring into steely life. I climb the ladder that is chipped lemon in the daytime and invisible in the night, a feel of aluminum rungs more than a ladder-being. "Power!" the lights blaze in the cockpit, undimmed by the little night-shields that close off most of their light for flying in the dark. The light from them shows me the parachute straps and the safety belt ends and the belt release lanyard and the G-suit and oxygen hoses and the microphone cables. Helmet on, oxygen mask on (how can rubber get so icy cold?), radio on. Night-shields down on the warning lights, twist the rheostats that fill the cockpit with a bloody glow. "Hawk Able Two," I say to the microphone, and if my flight leader has been faster strapping in than I, he will know that I am ready to go.

"Roj, Two." He is fast, my flight leader.

I do not know whether this is a real-thing alert or another practice. I assume it is another practice. Now I tend to the finer points of getting ready to go; checking circuit breakers in, bomb switches set in *safe* positions, gunsight properly set for the delivery that we will use.

"Hawk Able Four."

"Roj, Four."

Check the battle damage switches all down where they should be. Turn the navigation lights on to *bright flash*. We will turn them to *dim* as we approach the target.

"Hawk Able Three." Three was awake too late last night.

"Roj, Three. Parsnip, Hawk Able flight is ready to go with four."

In the combat operations center, the time is checked as we call in. We checked in well before the maximum time allowed, and this is good.

"Hawk Able, Parsnip here. This is a practice alert. Maintain cockpit alert until further notified."

"Roj."

So much meaning can be packed into three letters. Hawk Able Leader didn't just acknowledge the notice, he told the combat operations center that this is a ridiculous dumb stupid game to be played by grown men and good grief you guys it is THREE O'CLOCK IN THE MORNING and you had just better have orders from high headquarters to call this thing at this hour or you will not be getting much sleep tomorrow night.

"Sorry," says Parsnip, into the silence. They must have had the orders from high headquarters.

So I close the canopy and lock it against the eternal cold wind and I settle in the red light to wait.

I have waited fifteen minutes in the cockpit for the alert to be canceled. I have waited three hours for it. After the three-hour wait, I had climbed stiffly down from the cockpit with the perfect torture for recalcitrant prisoners of war. You take them and strap them by safety belt and shoulder harness to a soft, comfortable armchair. Then you walk away and leave them there. For the incorrigible prisoners, the real troublemakers, you put their feet into tunnels, sort of like rudder-pedal tunnels in a single-engine airplane, and put a control stick in the way so that they don't have room to move either foot into a different position. In a very few hours the prisoners will become docile, tractable, eager to mend their ways.

The sun isn't up yet. We wait in our cockpits. I drift idly in the great dark river of soft-flowing time. Nothing happens. The secondhand on my watch moves around. I begin to notice things; as something to do. I hear a quiet tik . . . tik . . . tik . . . very regular, slow, metronomic. Tik . . . tik . . . tik . . . And the answer comes. My navigation lights. Without the engine running and with the canopy closed to keep out the rustle of the wind, I can hear the opening and the closing of the relays that control the flashing of the lights on wingtip and tail. Interesting. Never would have thought that I could hear the lights going on and off.

Outside is the efficient high-speed pokpokpok of the APU. What a truly efficient thing that power unit is. It will stand there all night and through all tomorrow if it has to, pumping a constant stream of electricity to power the radio and keep the cockpit bathed in scarlet light.

My airplane rocks slightly. I think someone has climbed to the wing and wants to talk to me, but there is no one there. The wind, that gentle cold wind, rocks this massive hard airplane. Every once in a while, and faintly, the wind moves the airplane on its landing gear struts. Thirty feet to my right the airplane of Hawk Able Leader waits, lights on, tikking silently to itself. The bloodlight of the cockpit reflects from the foamwhite enameled helmet of the pilot just as it would reflect if we were cruising now at 30,000 feet. Canopy is closed and locked, the air inside the cockpit is still and cold, and I wish that someone would invent a way to pipe warm air into the cockpit of an airplane that waits in the cold of a very early day. I can feel my warmth being absorbed in the cold metal of the instrument panel and the ejection seat and canopy rails and rudder-pedal tunnels. If I could only be warm and move around a bit and have someone to talk to, sitting cockpit alert would not be too bad a thing.

I have made a discovery. This is what Lonely is. When you are walled up where no one can come inside and talk to you or play a game of cards or chess with you or share a joke about the time over Stuttgart when Number Three mistook the Moselle River for the Rhine and . . . Insulated from the outside. A truck that I know is a noisy line truck that clatters and squeaks and needs a new muffler glides noiselessly by on the road in front of my revetment. The locked canopy seals away the sound of its passing. It seals me in with my thoughts. Nothing to read, no moving things to watch, just a quiet cockpit and the tik of the nav lights and the pok of the APU and my very own thoughts.

I sit in an airplane that is mine. The commanders of Wing and Squadron have given it to me without question, trusting utterly in my ability to control it and guide it as they want it guided. They are depending on me to hit the target. I remember a line from the base newspaper that I read during a gigantic war game of a few weeks ago: "Yesterday the Wing saw action while it flew in support of the Army. . . ." The Wing did not see any such action. It was me that saw that action, arcing low and fast with simulated ordnance across the troops on the tanks, trying to streak low enough to make the troops jump into the mud but not low enough to take the whip antenna off the tanks.

Not the Wing making them jump.

Me.

Egoistical? Yes. But then the Wing did not take the chance of misjudging and driving its 12 tons of airplane into the side of a 50-ton armored tank. So this is me sitting Alert, in my airplane, and if it were a real Alert, it would be me who came back or did not come back from the flak and the missiles over the target. They trust me. That seems odd, that anyone should trust anyone else with so much. They give me an airplane without question and without thinking twice about it. The number of the airplane comes up by my name on the scheduling board and I go out and fly it or sit in its cockpit and be ready to fly it. It is just a number on the board. But when I sit in it I have a chance to see what a remarkably involved, what an intricately fashioned thing it is, and what power the commanders have given me by putting that number next to my name.

The crew chief, heavy-jacketed, steel-helmeted, appears abruptly on the aluminum ladder and knocks politely on the plexiglass. I open the canopy, grudging the loss of my pocket of still air, however slightly heated, to the cold wind, and pull one side of my helmet away from my ear so I can hear him. Red light paints his face.

"D'ymind if we climb in the truck and wait . . . be out of the wind a little bit if it's OK with you. Flash your taxi light if you need . . ."

"OK." And I resolve to discipline my thought and go over again the headings and the times and the distances and the altitudes to my target. And the great dark river of time moves slowly on.

As I sometimes have long moments for thought on the ground, so every once in a while there is a long cross-country flight that allows a moment to think and be alone with the sky and my airplane. And I smile. Alone with the airplane that has been called "the unforgiving F-84."

I have been waiting to fly the airplane that is unforgiving. There must be such an airplane somewhere that is so very critical that it must be flown exactly by the book or crash, for the word "unforgiving" appears often in the magazines racked in the pilots' lounges. But just when I think that the next type of airplane I am to fly has such high performance that it will be unforgiving, I learn to fly it. I learn its ways and its personality, and suddenly it is a forgiving airplane like all the others. It might be a little more critical on its airspeeds as I fly it down final approach to land, but as our acquaintance grows I discover that it has tolerances to either side of the best airspeed and that it will not spin into the ground if I am one knot too slow turning to the runway.

There is always a warning of danger, and only if a pilot fails to heed his airplane's warning will it go ahead and kill him.

The red fire-warning light comes on after takeoff. It could mean many things: a short circuit in the fire-warning system; too steep a climb at too low an airspeed; a hole in a combustion chamber wall; an engine on fire. Some airplanes have so much difficulty with false fire warnings that their pilots practically disregard them, assuming that the warning circuit has gone bad again. But the F-84F is not one of these; when the light comes on, the airplane is usually on fire. But still I have time to check it—to pull the throttle back, to climb to minimum ejection altitude, to drop the external stores, to check the tailpipe temperature and tachometer and fuel flow, to ask my wingman if he wouldn't mind taking a little look for smoke from my fuselage. If I am on fire, I have a few seconds to point the airplane away from the houses and bail out. I have never heard of an airplane that exploded without warning.

Jet airplanes are unforgiving in one common respect: they burn great quantities of fuel, and when the fuel is gone the engine stops running. Full tanks in a four-engine propeller-driven transport airplane can keep it in the air for 18 hours nonstop. Twin-engine cargo airplanes often have enough fuel aboard for eight hours of flying when they take off on a two-hour flight. But when I take off on an hour-forty-minute mission, I have enough fuel in the tanks of my '84F to last through two hours of flying. I do not have to concern myself with long minutes of circling in the air after the mission while other airplanes take off and land.

Occasionally I fly into the landing pattern with 300 pounds of JP-4 in the tanks, or enough for six minutes of flying at high power. If I was seven minutes from the runway with 300 pounds of fuel, I would not make it home with the engine running. If I was ten minutes from the runway, my wheels would never roll on that concrete again. If an airplane is disabled on the runway after I enter the landing pattern with six minutes of fuel, there had better be a fast tow truck waiting to pull it out of the way, or a second runway ready to be used. I will be coming to earth, in an airplane or in a parachute, within the next few minutes.

With the engine stopped, my airplane does not sink like a streamlined brick or a rock or a block of lead. It glides smoothly down, quietly down, as an airplane is designed to glide. I plan a deadstick pattern so that my wheels should touch half way down the runway, and I hold the landing gear retracted until I am certain that I am within gliding range of the field. Then, on final approach, with the runway long and white in the windscreen, it is gear down and flaps down and speed brakes out and emergency hydraulic pump on.

Though it is a hidden point of pride to have shut down the engine after a flight with 200 pounds of fuel remaining, tactical fighter pilots rarely give the required minimum fuel notice to the tower when they have less than 800 pounds remaining. The red low-level warning light may be blazing on the instrument panel near a fuel gage needle swinging down through 400 pounds, but unless it looks as if he will be delayed in his landing, the pilot does not call minimum fuel. He has pride in his ability to fly his airplane, and an unimportant thing like eight minutes of fuel remaining is not worthy of his concern.

A transport pilot once cut me out of the landing pattern by calling minimum fuel, receiving a priority clearance to land immediately. I had a full ten minutes of JP-4 in my main fuselage tank, so didn't mind giving way to the big airplane that needed to land so quickly. A week later I learned that the minimum fuel level set for that transport was thirty minutes of flying time; my engine could have flamed out three times over in the minutes before his fuel would have been really critical.

I respect the fact that my airplane burns fuel and that each flight ends without a great deal of fuel remaining, but it is a point of pride that I do this every day and that when I become concerned with the amount of fuel in my tanks, it is something that deserves concern.

It is a little, more than a little, like playing hooky from life, this airplane-flying business. I fly over the cities of France and Germany at ten o'clock in the morning and think of all the people down there who are working for a living while I pull my contrail free and effortlessly above them. It makes me feel guilty. I fly at 30,000 feet, doing what I enjoy doing more than anything else in all the world, and they are down there in the heat and probably not feeling godlike at all. That is their way. They could all have been fighter pilots if they had wished.

My neighbors in the United States used to look upon me a little condescendingly, waiting for me to grow out of the joy of flying airplanes, waiting for me to see the light and come to my senses and be practical and settle down and leave the Air Guard and spend my weekends at home. It has been difficult for them to believe that I will be flying so long as the Guard needs men in its airplanes, so long as there is an Air Force across the ocean that is training for war. So long as I think that my country is a pretty good place to live and should have the chance to go on being a pretty good place.

The cockpits of the little silver dots in front of the long white contrails are not manned only by the young and impractical. There is many an old fighter pilot still there; pilots who flew the Jugs and Mustangs and Spitfires and Messerschmitts of a long-ago war. Even the Sabre pilots and the Hog pilots of Korea are well-enough experienced to be called "old pilots," and they are the flight commanders and the squadron commanders of the operational American squadrons in Europe today. But the percentage changes a little every day, and for the most part the line pilots of NATO fighter squadrons have not been personally involved in a hot war.

There is a subtle feeling that this is not good; that the front-line pilots are not as experienced as they should be. But the only difference that exists is that the pilots since Korea do not wear combat ribbons on their dress uniforms.

Instead of firing on convoys filled with enemy troops, they fire on dummy convoys or make mock firing passes on NATO convoys in war games a few miles from the barbed-wire fence between East and West. And they spend hours on the gunnery ranges.

Our range is a small gathering of trees and grass and dust in the north of France, and in that gathering are set eight panels of canvas, each painted with a large black circle and set upright on a square frame. The panels stand in the sun and they wait.

I am one of the four fighter airplanes called Ricochet flight, and we come across the range on a spacing pass in close formation, echelon left. We fly a hundred feet above the dry earth, and each of the pilots of Ricochet flight is concentrating. Richochet Lead is concentrating on making this last turn smoothly, on holding his airspeed at 365 knots, on climbing a little to keep from scraping Ricochet Four into the next hill, on judging the point where he will break up and away from the other airplanes to establish a gunnery pattern for them to follow.

Ricochet Two is concentrating on flying as smoothly as he can, to give Three and Four the least amount of difficulty in flying their formation.

Ricochet Three flies watching only Lead and Two, intent on flying smoothly smoothly so that Four can stay in close to fly his position well.

And as Ricochet Four I think of staying in formation and of nothing else, so that the flight will look good to the range officer in his spotting tower. I am acutely conscious that every other airplane in the flight is doing his best to make the flying easy for me, and to thank them for their consideration I must fly so smoothly that the credit will be theirs. Each airplane flies lower than Ricochet Lead, and

Four flies closer to the ground than any of them. But to take even a half second to glance at the ground is to be a poor wingman. A wingman has complete total unwavering unquestioning faith in his leader. If Ricochet Lead flies too low now, if he doesn't pull the formation up a little to clear the hill, my airplane will be a sudden flying cloud of dirt and metal fragments and orange streamers of flame. But I trust the man who is flying as Ricochet Lead, and he inches the formation up to clear the hill and my airplane clears it as though it were a valley; I fly the position that I am supposed to fly and I trust the leader.

As Ricochet Four, I am stacked back and down to the left so that I can see up across the formation and line the white helmets of the other three pilots. That is all I should see and all I care to see: three helmets in three airplanes in one straight line. No matter what the formation does, I will stay with it in my position, keeping the three white helmets lined on each other. The formation climbs, it dives, it banks hard away from me, it banks toward me; my life is dedicated to do whatever is necessary with the throttle and the control stick and the rudder pedals and the trim button to stay in position and keep the helmets in line.

We are over the target panels and the radio comes to life.

"Ricochet Lead breaking right." The familiar voice that I know well; the voice, the words, the man, his family, his problems, his ambitions; is this instant the sudden flash of a swept silver wing pitching up and away to begin a pattern of gunnery practice, to develop a skill in a special brand of destruction. And I have only two helmets to line.

When Lead pitches away, Ricochet Two becomes the formation leader. His helmet flicks forward from watching the first airplane to look straight ahead, and he begins to count. One-thousand-one, one-thousand-two, one-thousand-*break!* With his own sudden flash of smooth metal wing, Ricochet Two disappears, and I have the luxuriously simple task of flying formation on only one airplane. Whose pilot is now looking straight ahead. One-thousand-one, one-thousand-two, one-thousand-*break!* The flash of wing happens to Three, only a few feet from my own wing, and I fly alone.

My head locks forward with Three's break, and I count. One-thousand-one isn't it a pretty day out today there are just a few clouds for a change and the targets will be easy to see. It is good to relax after that formation. Did a good job, though, Two and Three held it in well one-thousand-two good to have smooth air this morning. I won't have to worry about bouncing around too much when I put the pipper on the target. Today will be a good day for high scores. Let's see; sight is set and caged, I'll check the gun switch later with the other switches what a lonely place for someone to have to bail out. Bet there's no village for ten miles around one-thousand-*break!*

In my right glove the control stick slams hard to the right and back and the horizon twists out of sight. My G-suit inflates with hard air, pressing tightly into my legs and stomach. My helmet is heavy, but with a familiar heaviness that is not uncomfortable. The green hills pivot beneath me and I scan the brilliant blue sky to my right for the other airplanes in the pattern.

There they are. Ricochet Lead is a little swept dot two miles away turning onto base leg, almost ready to begin his first firing run. Two is a larger dot and level, following Lead by half a mile. Three is just now turning to follow Two; he is climbing and a thousand feet above me. And away down there is the clearing of the gunnery range and the tiny specks that are the strafing panels in the sun. I have all the time in the world.

Gun switch, beneath its red plastic guard, goes forward under my left glove to *guns,* sight is uncaged and set to zero angle of depression. The *gunfire* circuit breaker is pushed down under my right index finger. I twist the thick black throttle with my left glove to bring the computed range for the gunsight down to 1,000 feet. And my grip on the control stick changes.

With the gun switch off and the gunfire circuit breaker out, I fly formation holding the grip naturally, right index finger resting lightly on the red trigger at the front of the contoured plastic. Now, with guns ready to fire, the finger points straight ahead toward the instrument panel in an awkward but necessary position that keeps glove from touching trigger. The glove will stay off the trigger until I swing my airplane in a diving turn that brings the white dot on the sight reflector glass over the black dot painted on the strafing panel.

It is time to put the finishing touches on my attitude. I tell the audience behind my eyes that today I am going to shoot better than anyone else in this flight, that I will put at least 70 percent of my bullets into the black of the target, with the other 30 percent left to be scattered in the white cloth. I run through a picture of a good strafing attack in my mind; I see the black dot growing larger under the white dot of the gunsight, I see the sight-dot stay smoothly in the black, I feel the right index finger beginning to squeeze on the red trigger, I see the white now fully inside the black, I hear the muffled harmless sound of the guns firing their 50-caliber copperclad, and I see the powdered dust billow from behind the square of the target. A good pass.

But caution. Careful during the last seconds of the firing

run; don't become too concerned with putting a long burst into the cloth. I remember for a moment, as I always do before the first gunnery run of the day, the roommate of cadet days who let his enthusiasm fly his airplane a second too long, until his airplane and its target came sharply together on the ground. That is not a good way to die.

Power to 96 percent on the base leg, airspeed up to 300 knots, watch Three go in on his target.

"Ricochet Three's in, white and hot." And down he goes, a twisting silhouette of an '84F.

It is interesting to watch a firing pass from the air. There is no sound from the attacking airplane as it glides swiftly toward its target. Then, abruptly, grey smoke breaks noiselessly from the gunports at the nose of his airplane, streaming back to trace the angle of his dive in a thin smoky line. The dust of the ground begins to spray the air as the airplane breaks away, and a thick brown cloud of it billows at the base of the target when he is gone and climbing.

Now the only untouched target is target number four.

The warning panel on the ground by the spotting tower is turned red side down, white side up; the range is clear and safe for my pass. I note this, and fly along the base leg of the pattern, at right angle to my target. It is a mile away on the ground to my right. It drifts slowly back. It is at one o'clock low. It is at one-thirty low. I recheck the gun switch to *guns*. It is at two o'clock low and slam the stick whips to the right under my hand and my airplane rolls like a terrified animal and the sky goes grey with the G of the turn and the G-suit inflates to press me in a hard vise of trapped air. Beneath the canopy is pivoting blurred ground moving. It is the beginning of a good firing pass. The microphone button is down under my left thumb, "Ricochet Four is in, white and hot."

White and hot. The target is clear and the guns are ready to fire. Airspeed is up to 360 knots in the dive, and my wings roll level again. In the windscreen is a tiny square of white cloth with the speck of a black dot painted. I wait. The white dot called the pipper, the dot that shows on the windscreen where my bullets will converge, bounces in lazy slow bounces as it recovers from the sharp turn that began the pass. It settles down, and I touch the control stick back very gently in the dive so the pipper ambles up to cover the square of the target. And the target changes swiftly, as I wait, to become all things. It is an enemy tank waiting in ambush for the infantry; it is an antiaircraft gun that has let its camouflage slip; it is a black and puffing locomotive moving enemy supplies along a narrow-gage track. It is an ammunition dump a fortified bunker a truck towing a cannon a barge in the river an armored car and it is a white square of cloth with a black spot painted. It waits, I wait, and all of a sudden it grows. The spot becomes a disc, and the white pipper has been waiting for that. My finger squeezes slowly down on the red trigger. A gun camera starts as the trigger is half closed. Guns fire when the trigger is all the way down.

Like a rivet gun finishing a last-minute sheet metal job on the nose of the airplane, the guns sound; there is no ear-splitting roar and thunder and confusion in the cockpit. Just a little detached tututut while beneath my boots hot brass shell casings shower down into steel containers. I smell powder smoke in my oxgyen mask and idly wonder how it can find its way into a cabin that is supposed to be sealed and pressurized.

In ultra-slow motion I watch the target on the ground; it is serene and quiet, for the bullets have not yet arrived. The bullets are on the way, somewhere in the air between the blackening gunports on the nose of my airplane and the pulverized dust on the range. I once thought of bullets as being such fast things, and now I wait impatiently for them to touch the ground and verify my gunsight. Finger is off the trigger; a one-second burst is a long burst of fire. And there is the dust.

The ground comes apart and begins throwing itself into the air. A few feet short of the target the dust flies, but this means that many bullets will have found their way to the meeting point shown by the white dot in the center of the gunsight. The dust is still flying into the air as my right glove pulls back on the many-buttoned stick and my airplane climbs in the pattern. As my airplane and its shadow flick across the square of canvas, the bullets that are able to tear a concrete highway to impassible crushed rock still whip the air and rain on the ground. "Ricochet Four is off."

I bank to the right in the pattern and look back over my shoulder at the target. It is quiet now, and the cloud of dust is thinning in the wind and moving to the left, covering Three's target with a tenuous cloud of brown.

"Ricochet Lead is in."

I fired low that time, short of the target. There goes my 100 percent score. I must move the pipper up a little next time; place it on top of the disc of black. I smile at the thought. It is not very often that the air is smooth enough to let me think of placing the pipper inches high or inches low on the black spot of the target. I am normally doing very good to keep the pipper somewhere on the square of the strafing panel. But today is a good day for gunnery. Let the tanks beware the days of calm.

"Ricochet Two is in."

"Lead is off."

I watch Two, and in the curved plexiglass of the canopy

I see myself reflected as I watch; a Martian if I ever saw one. Hard white helmet, smooth-curved glare visor down and looking like a prop for a Man in Space feature, green oxygen mask covering all the face that the visor does not cover, oxygen hose leading down out of sight. No indication that there is a living thinking creature behind the hardware. The reflection watches Ricochet Two.

There it is, the grey wisp from the gunports in the nose. The target is still and waiting as though it will stand a year before seeing a sign of motion. Then, suddenly, the thick fountain of dust. To the left of the panel a twig on the ground jumps into startled life and leaps into the air. End over end, slowly it turns, shifting after its first instant into the familiar slow motion of things caught in the swift rain of machinegun bullets. It twists two full turns above the fountain and sinks gracefully back beneath the thick cloud of it. The concrete highway is torn to rock and the twig survives. That should carry a moral.

"Two is off." Smoke disappears from gunports. The airplane turns its oval nose to the sky and streaks away from the target.

"Three is in."

What is the moral of the twig? I think about it and I turn sharply into the base leg of the pattern, rechecking the gunsight, right index finger pointing forward at the altimeter. What is the moral of the twig?

The wisp of smoke trails from the gunports of the smooth aluminum nose of Ricochet Three, and I watch his pass.

There is no moral. If the target was a pile of twigs, the hail of copper and lead would turn it into a scattered blanket of splinters. This was a lucky twig. If you are a lucky twig, you can survive anything.

"Three is off."

The safety panel is white, the gun switch is at *guns*, and

[48]

slam the stick whips to the right under my glove and my airplane rolls like a terrified animal to the right and the sky goes grey with the G of the turn and the G-suit inflates to press me in a hard vise of trapped air.

I have never been so rushed, when I fly my airplane, that I do not think. Even in the gunnery pattern, when the air-speed needle is covering 370 knots and the airplane is a few feet from the ground, the thinking goes on. When events happen in split seconds, it is not the thinking that changes, but the event. Events fall obediently into slow motion when there is a need for more thought.

As I fly tonight, navigating with the TACAN locked firmly onto the Laon transmitter, there is plenty of time for thought, and obligingly, events telescope themselves so that seven minutes will pass in the moment between the haunted land of Abbeville and the TACAN transmitter at Laon, France. I do not pass time as I fly, time passes me.

The hills slip away. There is a solid layer of black cloud from the ground to within a thousand feet of my airplane. The ground is buried, but in my chariot of steel and aluminum and plexiglass I am carried above, and the stars are bright.

In the red light, on the windowed face of the radio-compass, are four selector knobs, one switch, and one coffee-grinder tuning crank. I turn the crank. It is as old-fashioned in the cockpit of a fighter plane as would be a hand-wound telephone in an atomic research center. If it was much more quiet and if I wore no helmet, perhaps I could hear the crank squeak as it turned. I turn the handle, imagining the squeaks, until the frequency needle comes to rest over the number 344, the frequency of the Laon radio-beacon.

Turn up the volume. Listen. Crank the handle a little to

the left, a little to the right. Static static crank dih-dih. Pause. Static. Listen for L-C. Dah-dih-dah-dih. . . . Dih-dah-dih-dih. . . . That is it. My right glove turns the selector from *antenna* to *compass,* while the left has the unnatural task of holding the control stick grip. The slim luminous green radiocompass needle spins majestically from the bottom of its dial to the top—a crosscheck on the TACAN —Laon radiobeacon is ahead. A little adjustment with the crank, an eighth of an inch, and the radiocompass is locked strong on Laon. Turn down the volume.

The Laon radiobeacon is a solitary place. It stands alone with the trees and the cold hills in the morning and the trees and the warm hills in the afternoon, sending its L-C into the air whether there is a pilot in the sky to hear it or whether there is nothing in the sky but a lone raven. But it is faithful and ever there. If the raven had a radiocompass, he could find his way unerringly to the tower that broadcasts the L-C. Every once in a long while a maintenance crew will go to the beacon and its tower and check its voltages and perform some routine tube-changing. Then they will leave the tower standing alone again and jounce back the rough road the way they came.

At this moment the steel of the tower is cold in the night and the raven is asleep in his stony home on a hillside. The coded letters, though, are awake and moving and alive, and I am glad, for the navigation is working out well.

The wide TACAN needle shares the same dial with the radiocompass needle, and they work together now to tell me that Laon is passing beneath my airplane. The radiocompass needle is the most active of the two. It twitches and quivers with stiff electronic life, like some deep sea life dredged and placed on a microscope slide. It jerks to the left and right; it quavers at the top of the dial, swinging in wider and wider arcs. Then, in one decisive movement, it swings all the way around, clockwise, and points to the bottom of the dial. The Laon radiobeacon has passed behind. The TACAN needle swings lazily five or six times around the dial and finally agrees with its more nervous companion. I am definitely past Laon.

That part of my thought that paid serious attention to navigation classes guides my glove to tilt the stick to the left, and the crowd of instruments in the center of the panel swings into an awareness of the seriousness of my action. Heading indicator moves on tiny oiled bearings to the left, turn needle leans to the left a quarter of an inch. The miniature airplane on the attitude indicator banks to the left against its luminous horizon line. Airspeed needle moves down a knot, altimeter and vertical speed needles drop for just a second, until I see their conspiracy and add the thought of back pressure through the right glove. The errant pair rise again into line.

Once again, the routine. Ready with the position report, thumb down on microphone button.

Though the cloud is almost at my flight level, and very dark, it looks as if the forecaster has once again gone astray, for I have not seen a flash of lightning since over the Channel. Whatever severe weather is afoot tonight over France is keeping itself well hidden. I am not concerned. In fifty minutes I shall be landing, with my precious sack of documents, at Chaumont.

CHAPTER THREE

"France Control, Air Force Jet Two Niner Four Zero Five, Laon." There is quiet static in the soft earphones. I wait. Perhaps my call went unnoticed.

"France Control, France Control, Jet Two Niner Four Zero Five, how do you read on frequency three one seven point eight." There is no answer.

It is not at all unusual for a radio to break down in flight, for radios are temperamental things. But it is never a comfortable feeling to fly at night above weather without some way of talking to the people on the ground. My glove moves to the right, to the frequency selector of the UHF command radio. I do not bother to watch it work, for it is simply changing a sliding square knob one click, from *manual* to *preset*. An indicator on the instrument panel juggles numbers in small windows, and finally decides to present the number 18, in small red-lit figures. In that one click I am aligned with a different set of people, away from the busy hub of the France Control Center to the quiet and pastoral surroundings of Calva Radar. I know that the stereotype is not a valid one, for radar stations are only smaller places than traffic control centers, and are often far more rushed and busy. Yet whenever I call a radar site, I feel a little more at ease, and imagine a small red brick building set in a field of brilliant green grass, with a cow grazing not far away.

"Calva Radar, Calva Radar, Air Force Jet Two Niner Four Zero Five, how do you read channel one eight." There is perhaps one chance in three that the UHF will work on this frequency when it did not work on the frequency for France Control. The cow outside the brick building is asleep, a sculptured boulder in the dark of the grass. A light is in the window of the building, and a man's shadow moves across the glass as he reaches for his microphone.

". . . ero five . . . . d you . . . . . arbled . . . . . Calva?"

The UHF is definitely on its way out of commission. But even if it goes completely out, I am still cleared to maintain flight level 330 all the way to the Chaumont TACAN holding pattern. There are occasional moments like this when I wish that the airplane had just one more communication radio installed. But the F-84F was built for fighting, not for talking, and I must make do with what I have.

"Calva Radar, Four Zero Five unable to contact France Control, was Laon at one zero, flight level three three zero assigned instrument flight rules, estimating Spangdahlem at two eight, Wiesbaden." A wild try. A shot in the dark. But at least the information was said, and I have made the required report. I hear Calva's microphone button go down.

[53]

". . . ive . . . ort . . . . . mly garb . . . . come up . . . point zero . . ."

Calva is suggesting another frequency, but by the time I can understand all of his message I will be too far away for it to matter. Trying to send a position report with a radio in this condition is like trying to shout a message across a deep and windy chasm; difficult and frustrating. I give my report once again to comply with the rules, click back to *manual* and forget the matter. Too bad. It would have been good to hear the latest weather report along my route, but simply getting my request understood would have been a major problem, to say nothing of receiving a reply. The weather is of only academic interest anyway, for there would have to be a pilot report of a squall line with severe turbulence and heavy icing to 40,000 feet before I would consider turning back.

I look back over my left shoulder as I turn to the heading that will take me to Spangdahlem.

I am pulling a contrail.

In a sweeping turn behind me, following like a narrow wake of a high-speed racing boat, is a twisting tunnel of glowing grey mist in the starlight that is the path that I have followed. Clearly and precisely in texts on atmospheric physics, contrails are explained by the men who spend their time with radio balloons and diagrams of the upper air.

Contrails are like fireflies. If I desire, I can find pages of explanation about them in books and in specialized magazines. But when I see one close at hand, it is alive and mystic and greyly luminous. Watching the con as I turn, I can see the rise and fall of it where I made small changes to keep my airplane at flight level 330. It looks like a very gentle roller-coaster, one for people who do not like excitement. That is where I have been. No air aside from the rolling tunnel of mist can say that it has felt my passage. If I desire, I can turn now and fly through exactly the same air that I flew before. And I am alone. As far as I can see, and that is a long distance about me, there is no other contrail in the sky. I am the only person in all the world to fly above the clouds in the hundreds of cubic miles that make the world of high altitude between Abbeville and Spangdahlem this evening. It is a solitary feeling.

But there is work to be done. Back to the coffee grinder. Squeak squeak to frequency 428. Volume up. Static. And no second thoughts, no mistaking this one. An S and a P and an A. A city with its thousands of people, with the cares and the joys that they share, people, with me. I am alone and six miles above their earth, and their city is not even a light grey glow in the black cloud. Their city is an S and a P and an A in the soft earphones. Their city is the needlepoint at the top of the dial.

The frequency selector knob of the TACAN set clicks under my right glove to channel 100, and after a moment of indecision, the modern, smoothworking mileage drum spins to show 110 miles to the Spangdahlem beacon. Except for the failure of the UHF radio, my flight has gone very smoothly. There is a faint flicker in the rising hills of cloud far ahead to my right, as if someone is having difficulty striking an arc with a gigantic welding rod. But distances at night are deceiving, and the flash of light could be over any one of four countries.

As a pilot, I have traveled and seen millions of square miles of land and cloud above land. As a recalled Guard pilot in Europe I have rolled my wheels on hundreds of miles of asphalt and concrete runways in seven countries. I can say that I have seen more of the continent than many

[55]

people, yet Europe is a much different place for me than it is for them. It is a patterned country, broad and wide in the sunlight, wrinkled in the south by the Pyrenees and in the east by the Alps. It is a country over which someone has spilled a great sack of airports, and I seek these out.

France is not the France of travel posters. France is Etain Air Base and Chateauroux Air Base and Chaumont and Marville. It is the patchwork of Paris about its beloved river, a patchwork that flows like crystallized lava around the tictactoe runways of Orly Field and Le Bourget. France is the repetition of walking over the concrete to Base Operations and being aware, as I walk, of tiny villages outside the perimeter fence and hills everywhere.

Europe is a pitifully small place. From 37,000 feet above the Pyrenees I can see the cold Atlantic at Bordeaux and the shores of the French Riviera on the Mediterranean. I can see Barcelona, and in the haze, Madrid. In thirty minutes I can fly over England, Holland, Luxembourg, Belgium, France, and Germany. My squadron flies nonstop to North Africa in two and a half hours; it patrols the border between West and East in Germany; can fly to Copenhagen for the weekend. So this was a school for mankind. A small schoolyard.

But I rarely get first-hand, visual evidence of the postage stamp that is Europe, for much more often than not the land is covered by tremendous decks of cloud, seas of white and grey that stretch without a rift from horizon to horizon. It is the weather in Europe, as in the United States, that reminds me now and then that, although I can span continents in a single leap, I am not always so godlike as I feel. Some clouds in summer tower past my airplane to 50,000 feet, and some boil up and build faster than my airplane can climb. Much of the time I am correct in saying that mine is an over-the-weather airplane, but clouds are watch-keepers over arrogant men, they remind me, just often enough, of my actual size.

The swirling masses of white cumulus will some days harbor only the mildest of turbulence along my path. Another day I may penetrate the same type of cloud and come out of it grateful to the man who designed the crash helmet. Tight as safety belt and shoulder harness can be, it is still in the province of a few clouds to snap my helmet sharply against the canopy and flex the steelspar wings that I once swore could never be forced an inch.

I was once constantly wary of the hardest-looking clouds, but I have learned that, despite the snap of helmet on canopy, their turbulence is rarely strong enough to really damage a fighter airplane. Every once in a while I read of a multiengine airplane that lost its windshield or radome in the hail, or has taken a bolt or two of lightning, for these instances are duly reported and photographed in detail for the pilots' magazines. There are a few airplanes that have taken off into bad weather, into thunderstorms, and have been found days later or weeks later scattered across a lonely stretch of earth. The reasons are unknown. The storm might have been unusually powerful; the pilot could have lost control; he could have been caught in a web of vertigo and dived from storm into ground. So, although my airplane has a six-layer bulletproof windscreen designed for worse than hail and an airframe stressed to withstand twice the force that would tear the wings from larger airplanes, I respect thunderstorms. I avoid them when I can; I grit my teeth and hold on to the control stick when I can't. So far, I have been knocked about by a few small thunderstorms, but I have not seen them all.

There are procedures, of course. Tighten the safety belt

and shoulder harness, pitot heat and defrosters on, cockpit lights to full bright, airspeed down to 275 knots, and try to hold the airplane level. In the vertical air currents of a thunderstorm, altimeters and vertical speed indicators and even airspeed indicators are practically useless. They lag and they lead and they flutter helplessly. Though the '84F tends to yaw and roll a bit in turbulence, I must try to fly by the little airplane on a two-inch gyrostabilized horizon set ahead of me on the instrument panel: the attitude indicator. I fly to hold my attitude straight and level through the storm. So I am prepared. I always have been.

In the darkness of the French night, my airplane flies easily along the continuous stream of miles between Laon and Spangdahlem, through air as smooth as polished obsidian. I tilt my white helmet back against the red ejection seat headrest and look up from the thick dark layer of cloud to the deeper, bright layer of stars overhead, that have so long guided men across the earth. The constant, eternal stars. The reassuring stars. The useless stars. In an airplane like mine, built to work at its best through a pilot's eyes and a pilot's direction, the stars have become only interesting spots of light to look out upon when all is going well. The important stars are the ones that draw the luminous needles of the radiocompass and the TACAN. Stars are nice, but I navigate by the S and the P and the A.

Tactical fighter pilots have traditionally been on marginal terms with the thought of weather flying, and only by superhuman efforts has the Air Force brought them to accept the thought that nowadays even fighter airplanes must fly in weather. The official emphasis takes the form of motion pictures and ground schools and instrument schools and required minimum hours of instrument and hooded flight every six months. Each successive fighter airplane becomes more capable of operating in all-weather conditions, and today interceptor pilots in their big delta-wings can fly a complete interception and attack on an enemy airplane without ever seeing it except as a smoky dot of light on their attack radar screen.

Even the fighter-bomber, long at the mercy of the low cloud, is today capable of flying a low-level attack through the weather, using sophisticated radar systems in order to avoid the hard mountains and identify the target. Beyond the official emphasis and the pressure of regulations, tactical fighter pilots of the newest airplanes must learn all there is to know about weather flying simply to keep up with their airplane, to be able to use it as it was meant to be used. But weather is still an enemy. The cloud robs me of the horizon and I cannot see outside the cockpit. I am forced to depend completely on seven expressionless faces in glass that are my flight instruments. There is, in weather, no absolute up or down. There is only a row of instruments that say, *this is up, this is down, this is the horizon.* When so much of my flying is done in the clear world of air-to-ground gunnery, it is not easy to stake my life on the word of a two-inch circle of glass and radium paint, yet that is the only way to stay alive after my airplane sinks into cloud. The feel and the senses that hold the pipper steady on the tank are easily confused when the world outside is a faceless flow of grey.

After a turn, or after the harmless movement of tilting my head to look at the radio set as I change frequencies, those senses can become shocked and panic-stricken, can shout *you're diving to the left!* although the gyro horizon is a calm and steady guide on the instrument panel. Caught in the contradiction, I have a choice: follow one voice or follow the other. Follow the sense that marks me *expert* in strafe and rocket and high-angle dive-bomb, or follow the little bit of tin and glass which someone has told me is the thing to trust.

I follow the tin, and a war is on. Vertigo has become so strong that I have had to lean my helmet almost to my shoulder in accord with its version of up and down. But still I fly the instruments. Keep the little tin airplane level in its glass *you're banking hard to the right* keep the altimeter and vertical speed needles steady *look out, you're starting to dive* . . . keep the turn needle straight up and the ball in the center of its curved glass tube *you're rolling! you're upside down and you're rolling!* Keep crosschecking the instruments. One to the next to the next to the next.

The only common factor between combat flying and instrument flying is one of discipline. I do not break away from my leader to seek a target on my own; I do not break away from the constant clockwise crosscheck of the seven instruments on the black panel in front of me. The discipline of combat is usually the easier. There I am not alone, I can look out and see my leader and I can look up and back to see the second element of my flight, waiting to go in and fire on the enemy.

When the enemy is an unresisting grey fog, I must rely on the instruments and pretend that this is just another practice flight under the canvas instrument hood over the rear cockpit of a T-33 jet trainer, that I can lift the hood any time that I would like, and see a hundred miles of clear air in all directions. I am just not concerned with lifting the hood. Weather, despite the textbook familiarity that ground schools give and that experience reinforces, is still my greatest enemy. It is difficult to predict exactly, and worse, it is completely uncaring of the men and the machines that fly into it. It is completely uncaring.

"Air Force Jet Two Niner Four Zero Five, France Control with an advisory." Like a telephone ringing. My radio. There is not the slightest flaw in its operation. How can that be when only a minute ago . . . but it is working now and that is all that matters. Microphone button down. Professional voice.

"Roger, France; Four Zero Five, go."

"Four Zero Five, Flight Service advised mutiengine aircraft reports severe turbulence, hail and heavy icing in vicinity of Phalsbourg. Also T-33 reported moderate turbulence at flight level three zero zero, light clear icing."

Button down. What about that. Sounds as if there might be a thunderstorm or two in the stratus ahead. That was in the textbook, too. But still it is rare to have very large thunderstorms in France. "Roger, France, thank you for the advisory. What is the current weather at Chaumont?"

"Stand by one."

I stand by, waiting while another man in a white shirt and loose tie riffles through his teletyped weather reports looking for the one out of hundreds that is coded LFQU. With one hand he sorts and moves the weather from the Continent over; he shuffles through rain and haze and fog and high cloud and winds and ice and blowing dust. He is at this moment touching the sheet of yellow paper that tells him, if he wants to read it, that Wheelus Air Base, Libya, has clear skies with visibilities to 20 miles and a 10-knot wind from the southwest. If he wants to know, a line on the paper tells him that Nouasseur, Morocco, is calling high broken cirrus, visibility 15 miles, wind west southwest at 15 knots. He thumbs through weather from Hamburg (measured 1,200-foot overcast, visibility three miles in rain showers, wind from the northwest at ten knots) from Wiesbaden Air Base (900-foot overcast, visibility two miles, wind from the south at seven knots), from Chaumont Air Base.

"Jet Two Niner Four Zero Five, Chaumont is calling a measured one thousand one hundred foot overcast, visibility four miles in rain, winds from the southwest at one zero gusting one seven." The weather at Chaumont is neither good nor bad.

"Thank you very much, France." The man clicks his microphone button in reply. He lets the thick sheaf of yellow paper pile upon itself again, covering with its weight the weather of hundreds of airports across the Continent. And cover the report from Phalsbourg Air Base (measured ceiling 200 feet, visibility one half mile in heavy rain showers, wind from the west at 25 gusting 35 knots. Cloud-to-cloud, cloud-to-ground lightning all quadrants, one-half-inch hail).

I drift along above the slanting cloud as if reality were all a dream with fuzzy soft edges. The starlight falls and soaks into the upper few feet of the mist, and I relax in a deep pool of red light and look out at the cold idyllic world that I called, when I was a boy, Heaven.

I can tell that I am moving. I do not have to accept that with my intellect as the radiocompass needle swings from one beacon to the next and the mileage drum of the distance measuring equipment unrolls. I see smooth waves of cloud pull darkly silently by a few hundred feet beneath my airplane. A beautiful night to fly.

What was that? What did I say? Beautiful? That is a word for the weak and the sentimental and the dreamers. That is not a word for the pilots of 23,000 pounds of tailored destruction. That is not a word to be used by people who watch the ground disintegrate when they move their finger, or who are trained to kill the men of other countries whose Heaven is the same as their own. Beautiful. Love. Soft. Delicate. Peace. Stillness. Not words or thoughts for fighter pilots, trained to unemotion and coolness in emergency and strafe the troops on the road. The curse of sentimentality is a strong curse. But the meanings are always there, for I have not yet become a perfect machine.

In the world of man/airplane, I live in an atmosphere of understatement. The wingman pulling a scarlet contrail in the sunset is kinda pretty. Flying fighters is a pretty good job. It was too bad about my roommate flying into his target.

One learns the language, what is allowed to be said and what is not. I discovered, a few years ago, that I was not different from all the other pilots when I caught myself thinking that a wingman and his contrail in the last light of the sun is not a single thing but beautiful, or that I love my airplane, or that my country is a country for which I would gladly lay down my life. I am not different.

I learn to say, "Single-engine flying is all right, I guess," and any other pilot in the Air Force knows exactly that I am as proud to be a jet fighter pilot as anyone is proud of any job, anywhere. Yet nothing could be more repelling than the term "jet fighter pilot." *Jet*. Words for movie posters and nonpilots. *Jet* means glamour and glory and the artifical chatter of a man who wishes he knew something of fighter airplanes. *Jet* is an embarrassing word. So I say *single-engine,* for the people I speak with know what I mean: that I have the chance to be off and alone with the clouds every once in a while, and if I want, I can fly faster than sound or knock a tank off its tracks or turn a roundhouse into a pile of bricks and hot steel under a cloud of black smoke. Flying jets is a mission for supermen and superheros dashing handsome movie actors. Flying single-engine is just a pretty good job.

The white jagged fence of the Alps was not a fence to a Fox Eight Four, and we had ambled across them at altitude almost as uncaring as the gull that floats above the predators of the sea. Almost. The mountains, even under their tremendous blanket, were sharp, like great shards of splintered glass on a snowy desert. No place at all for an engine failure. Their spiny tops jutted above the stratus sea in the ancient way that led one pilot to call them "Islands in the Sky." Hard rock islands above soft grey cotton sea. Silence on the radio. I flew wing silently, watching the islands drift below. Three words from the flight leader. "Rugged, aren't they?"

We have together been watching the islands. They are the most tortured masses of granite and pending avalanche in the world. Raw world upthrust. A virgin treacherous land of sliding snow and falling death. An adventure-world for the brave and the superhumans who climb because they are there. No place at all for a bewilderingly human thing called an airplane pilot and depending on a great many spinning steel parts to go on spinning in order that he might stay in the sky. That he loves.

"Roj," I say. What else was there to say? The mountains were rugged.

It is always interesting. The ground moves below, the stars move overhead, the weather changes, and rarely, very rarely, one of the ten thousand parts that is the body of an airplane fails to operate properly. For a pilot, flying is never dangerous, for a man must be a little bit insane or under the press of duty to willingly remain in a position that he truly considers dangerous. Airplanes occasionally crash, pilots are occasionally killed, but flying is not dangerous, it is interesting.

It would be nice, one day, to know which of my thoughts are mine alone and which of them are common to all the people who fly fighter airplanes.

Some pilots speak their thoughts by long habit, some say nothing at all of them. Some wear masks of convention and imperturbability that are very obvious masks, some wear masks so convincing that I wonder if these people are not really imperturbable. The only thoughts that I know are my own. I can predict how I will control my own mask in any number of situations. In emergencies it will be forced into a nonchalant calm that is calculated to rouse admiration in the heart of anyone that hears my unruffled voice on the radio. That, for one, is not strictly my own device. I talked once with a test pilot who told me his way of manufacturing calm in emergencies. He counts to ten out loud in his oxygen mask before he presses the microphone button to talk to anyone. If the emergency is such that he does not have ten seconds to count, he is not interested in talking to anyone; he is in the process of bailing out. But in lesser emergencies, by the time he has counted to ten, his voice has accustomed itself to a background of emergency, and comes as smoothly over the radio as if he were giving a pilot report on the tops of some fair-weather cumulus clouds.

There are other thoughts of which I do not speak. The destruction that I cause on the ground. It is not in strict accord with the Golden Rule to fly down an enemy convoy and tear its trucks to shreds with six rapid-fire heavy machine guns, or to drop flaming jellied gasoline on the men or to fire 24 high-explosive rockets into their tanks or to loft an atomic bomb into one of their cities. I do not talk about that. I rationalize it out for myself, until I hit upon a certain reasoning that allows me to do all these things without a qualm. A long while ago I found a solution that is logical and true and effective.

The enemy is evil. He wants to put me into slavery and he wants to overrun my country, which I love very much. He wants to take away my freedom and tell me what to think and what to do and when to think and when to do it. If he wants to do this to his own people, who do not mind the treatment, that is all right with me. But he will not do that to me or to my wife or to my daughter or to my country. I will kill him before he does.

So those legged dots streaming from the stalled convoy beneath my guns are not men with thoughts and feelings and loves like mine; they are evil and they mean to take my way of life from me. The tank is not manned by five frightened human beings who are praying their own special kind of prayers as I begin my dive and put the white dots of the gunsight pipper on the black rectangle that is their tank; they are evil and they mean to kill the people that I love.

Thumb lightly on the rocket button, white dot on black rectangle, thumb down firmly. A light, barely audible swish-swish from under my wings and four trails of black smoke angle down to converge on the tank. Pull up. A little shudder as my airplane is passed by the shock waves of the rocket explosions. They are evil.

I am ready for whatever mission I am assigned. But flying is not all the grim business of war and destruction and rationalized murder. In the development of man/machine, events do not always conform to plan, and flight shacks and ready rooms are scattered with magazines of the business of flying that point up the instances when man/machine did not function as he was designed.

Last week I sat in a soft red imitation-leather armchair in the pilots' lounge and read one of those well-thumbed magazines from cover to cover. And from it, I learned.

A pair of seasoned pilots, I read, were flying from France to Spain in a two-seat Lockheed T-33 jet trainer. Half an hour from their destination, the pilot in the rear seat reached down to the switch that controls his seat height, and inadvertently pressed the release that fires a blast of high-pressure carbon dioxide to inflate the one-man rubber liferaft packed into his ejection seat cushion. The raft ballooned to fill the rear cockpit, smashing the hapless pilot tightly against his seat belt and shoulder harness.

This had happened before with liferafts, and in the cockpits of the airplanes that carry them is a small sharp knife blade to use in just such emergencies. The rear-seat pilot reached the blade, and in a second the raft exploded in a dense burst of carbon dioxide and talcum powder.

The front-seat pilot, carrying on the business of flying the airplane and unaware of the crisis behind him, heard the boom of the raft exploding and instantly his cockpit was filled with talcum powder, which he assumed to be smoke.

When you hear an explosion and the cockpit fills with smoke, you do not hesitate, you immediately cut off the fuel to the engine. So the front-seat pilot slammed the throttle to *off* and the engine stopped.

In the confusion, the pilot in back had disconnected his microphone cable, and assumed that the radio was dead. When he saw that the engine had flamed out, he pulled his

[67]

ejection seat armrests up, squeezed the steel trigger and was blown from the airplane to parachute safely into a swamp. The other pilot stayed with the trainer and successfully crash-landed in an open field.

It was a fantastic train of errors, and my laugh brought a question from across the room. But as I told what I had read, I tucked it away as a thing to remember when I flew again in either seat of the squadron T-33.

When my class of cadets was going through flying training, just beginning our first rides in the T-33, our heads were filled with memorized normal procedures and emergency procedures until it was not an easy thing to keep them all straight. It was bound to happen to someone, and it happened to Sam Wood. On his very first morning in the new airplane, with the instructor strapped into the rear cockpit, Sam called, "Canopy clear?" warning the other man that a 200-pound canopy would be pressed hydraulically down on the rails an inch from his shoulders.

"Canopy clear," the instructor said. Sam pulled the canopy jettison lever. There was a sudden, sharp concussion, a cloud of blue smoke, and 200 pounds of curved and polished plexiglass shot 40 feet into the air and crashed to the concrete parking ramp. Sam's flight that day was canceled.

Problems of this sort plague the Air Force. The human part of the man/airplane has just as many failures as the metal part, and they are more difficult to troubleshoot. A pilot will fly 1,500 hours in many kinds of airplanes, and is said to be experienced. On the landing from his 1,501st flight hour, he forgets to extend his landing gear and his airplane slides in a shower of sparks along the runway. To prevent gear-up landings there have been many inventions and many thousands of words and warnings written.

When a throttle is pulled back to less than minimum power needed to sustain flight, a warning horn blows in the cockpit and a red light flares in the landing gear lowering handle. This means "Lower the wheels!" But habit is a strong thing. One gets used to hearing the horn blowing for a moment before the wheels are lowered on each flight, and gradually it becomes like the waterfall that is not heard by the man who lives in its roar. There is a required call to make to the control tower as the pilot turns his airplane onto base leg in the landing pattern: "Chaumont Tower, Zero Five is turning base, gear down, pressure up, brakes checked." But the call becomes habit, too. Sometimes it happens that a pilot is distracted during the moment that he normally spends moving the landing gear lever to the *down* position. When his attention is again fully directed to the job of landing his airplane, his wheels should be down and he assumes they are. He glances at the three lights that show landing gear position, and though not one of them glows the familiar green, though the light in the handle is shining red and the warning horn is blowing, he calls, "Chaumont Tower, Zero Five is turning base, gear down, pressure up, brakes checked."

The inventors took over and tried to design the human error out of their airplanes. Some airspeed indicators have flags that cover the dial during a landing approach unless the wheels are down, on the theory that if the pilot cannot read his airspeed he will be shocked into action, which here involves lowering the gear. In the deadliest, most sophisticated interceptor in the air today, that carries atomic missiles and can kill an enemy bomber under solid weather conditions at altitudes to 70,000 feet, there is a landing gear warning horn that sounds like a high-speed playback of a wide-range piccolo duet. The inventors deduced that if this wild noise would not remind a pilot to lower his landing gear, they were not going to bother with lights or covering the airspeed indicator or any other tricks; he would be beyond them all. When I see one of the big grey delta-wing interceptors in the landing pattern, I am forced to smile at the reedy tootling that I know the pilot is hearing from his gear warning horn.

Suddenly, in my dark cockpit, the thin luminous needle of the radiocompass swings wildly from its grip on the Spangdahlem radiobeacon and snaps me from my idle thoughts to the business of flying.

The needle should not move. When it begins to swing over Spangdahlem, it will first make very small leftright quivers on its card to warn me. The leftrights will become wider and wider and the needle will finally turn to point at the bottom of the dial, as it did passing Laon.

But the distance-measuring drum shows that I am still 40 miles from my first German checkpoint. The radiocompass has just warned me that it is a radiocompass like all the others. It was designed to point the way to centers of low-frequency radio activity, and there is no more powerful center of low-frequency radio activity than a fully-grown thunderstorm. For years I have heard the rule of thumb and applied it: stratus clouds mean stable air and smooth flying. In an aside to itself, the rule adds (except when there are thunderstorms hidden in the stratus).

Now, like a boxer pulling on his gloves before a fight, I reach to my left and push the switch marked *pitot heat*. On the right console is a switch with a placard *windscreen defrost* and my right glove flicks it to the *on* position, lighted in red by hidden bulbs. I check that the safety belt is as tight as I can pull it, and I cinch the shoulder harness straps a quarter of an inch tighter. I have no intention of deliberately flying into a thunderstorm tonight, but the padlocked canvas sack in the gun bay ahead of my boots reminds me that my mission is not a trifling one, and worth a calculated risk against the weather.

The radiocompass needle swings again, wildly. I look for the flicker of lightning, but the cloud is still and dark. I have met a little rough weather in my hours as a pilot, why should the contorted warning feel so different and so ominous and so final? I note my heading indicator needle steady on my course of 084 degrees, and, from habit, check it against the standby magnetic compass. The gyro-held needle is within a degree of the incorruptible mag compass. In a few minutes the cloud will reach up to swallow my airplane, and I shall be on instruments, and alone.

It is a strange feeling to fly alone. So much of my flying is done in two- and four-ship formations that it takes time for the loneliness to wear from solo flight, and the minutes between Wethersfield and Chaumont Air Base are not that long a time. It is unnatural to be able to look in any direction that I wish, throughout an entire flight. The only comfortable position, the only natural position, is when I am looking 45 degrees to the left or 45 degrees to the right, and to see there the smooth streamlined mass of the lead airplane, to see the lead pilot in his white helmet and dark visor looking left and right and up and behind, clearing the flight from other airplanes in the sky and occasionally looking back for a long moment at my own airplane. I watch my leader more closely than any first violin watches his conductor, I climb when he climbs, turn when he turns, and watch for his hand signals.

Formation flying is a quiet way to travel. Filling the air with radio chatter is not a professional way of accomplishing a mission, and in close formation, there is a hand signal to cover any command or request from the leader and the answer from his wingman.

It would be easier, of course, for the leader to press his microphone button and say, "Gator flight: speed brakes . . . now," than to lift his right glove from the stick, fly with his left for a second while he makes the thumb-and-fingers speed brake signal, put his right glove back on the stick while Gator Three passes the signal to Four, put his left glove on the throttle with thumb over sawtooth speed brake switch above the microphone button, then nod his helmet suddenly and sharply forward as he moves the switch under his thumb to *extend*. It is more complicated, but it is more professional, and to be professional is the goal of every man who wears the silver wings over his left breast pocket.

It is professional to keep radio silence, to know all there is to know about an airplane, to hold a rock-solid position in any formation, to be calm in emergencies. Everything that is desirable about flying airplanes is "professional." I joke with the other pilots about the extremes to which the word is carried, but it cannot really be overused, and I honor it in my heart.

I work so hard to earn the title of a professional pilot that I come down from each close-formation flight wringing wet with sweat; even my gloves are wet after a flight, and dry into stiff wrinkled boards of leather before the next day's mission. I have not yet met the pilot who can fly a good formation flight without stepping from his cockpit as though it was a swimming pool. Yet all that is required for a smooth, easy flight is to fly a loose formation. That, however, is not professional, and so far I am convinced that the man who lands from a formation flight in a dry flight suit is not a good wingman. I have not met that pilot and I probably never will, for if there is one point in which all single-engine pilots place their professionalism in open view, it is in formation flying.

At the end of every mission, there is a three-mile initial approach to the landing pattern, in close echelon formation. In the 35 seconds that it takes to cover those three miles, from the moment that the flight leader presses his microphone button and says, "Gator Lead turning initial runway one niner, three out with four," every pilot on the flight line and scores of other people on the base will be watching the formation. The flight will be framed for a moment in the window of the commander's office, it will be in plain sight from the Base Exchange parking lot, visitors will watch it, veteran pilots will watch it. It is on display for three miles. For 35 seconds it is the showpiece of the entire base.

I tell myself that I do not care if every general in the United States Air Force in Europe is watching my airplane, or if just a quail is looking up at me through the tall grass. The only thing that matters is the flight, the formation. Here is where I tuck it in. Every correction that I make will be traced in the grey smoke of my exhaust and will be one point off the ideal of four straight grey arrows with unmoving sweptsilver arrowheads. The smallest change means an immediate correction to keep the arrow straight.

I am an inch too far from the leader; I think the stick to the left and recover the inch. I bounce in the rough afternoon air; I move it in on the leader so that I bounce in the same air that he does. Those 35 seconds require more concentrated attention than all the rest of the flight. During a preflight briefing, the leader can say, ". . . and on initial, let's just hold a nice formation; don't press it in so close that you feel uncomfortable . . ." but every pilot in the flight smiles to himself at the words and knows that when that half-minute comes, he will be just as uncomfortable as the other wingmen in the closest, smoothest formation that he can fly.

The tension in those seconds builds until I think that I cannot hold my airplane so close for one more second. But the second passes and so does another, with the green glass of my leader's right navigation light inches from my canopy.

At last he breaks away in a burst of polished aluminum into the landing pattern, and I begin the count to three. I follow him through the pattern and I wait. My wheels throw back their long plumes of blue smoke on the hard runway and I wait. We taxi back to the flight line in formation and we shut down our engines and we fill out the forms and we wait. We walk back to the flight shack together, parachute buckles tinkling like little steel bells, waiting. Occasionally it comes. "Looked pretty good on initial today, Gator," someone will say to the lead pilot.

"Thanks," he will say.

I wonder in an unguarded moment if it is worth it. Is it worth the work and the sweat and sometimes the danger of extremely close formation flying just to look good in the approach? I measure risk against return, and have an answer before the question is finished and phrased. It is worth it. There are four-ship flights making approaches to this runway all day long, seven days a week. To fly one approach so well that it stands out in the eye of a man who watches hundreds of them is to fly an outstanding piece of formation. A professional formation. It is worth it.

If day formation is work, then night formation is sheer travail. But there is no more beautiful mission to be found in any Air Force.

Lead's airplane melts away to join the black sky and I

fly my number Three position on his steady green navigation light and the faint red glow that fills his cockpit and reflects dimly from his canopy. Without moon or starlight, I can see nothing whatsoever beyond his lights, and take the thought on slimmest faith that there is 10 tons of fighter plane a few feet from my cockpit. But I usually have the starlight.

I drift along on Lead's wing with my engine practicing its balky V-8 imitation behind me and I watch the steady green light and the dim red glow and the faint faint silhouette of his airplane under the stars. At night the air is smooth. It is possible, at altitude and when Lead is not turning, to relax a little and compare the distant lights of a city to the nearer lights that are the stars around me. They are remarkably alike.

Distance and night filter out the smallest lights of the city, and altitude and thin clear air bring the smallest of stars into tiny untwinkling life. Without an undercast of cloud, it is very difficult to tell where sky ends and ground begins, and more than one pilot has died because the night was perfectly clear. There is no horizon aside from the ever-faithful one two inches long behind its disc of glass on the panel with its 23 comrades.

At night, from 35,000 feet, there is no fault in the world. There are no muddy rivers, no blackened forests, nothing except silver-grey perfection held in a light warm shower of starlight. I know that the white star painted on Lead's fuselage is dulled with streaks of oil rubbed by dusty rags, but if I look very closely I can see a flawless five-pointed star in the light of the unpointed stars through which we move.

The *Thunderstreak* looks very much as it must have looked in the mind of the man who designed it before he got down to the mundane task of putting lines and numbers on paper. A minor work of art, unblemished by stenciled black letters that in day read *fire ingress door* and *cradle pad* and *danger—ejection seat*. It looks like one of the smooth little company models in grey plastic, without blemish or seam.

Lead dips his wing sharply to the right, blurring the green navigation light in a signal for Two to cross over and take the position that I now fly on Lead's right wing. With Four floating slowly up and down in the darkness off my own right wing, I inch back my throttle and slide gently out to leave an '84-size space for Two. His navigation lights change from *bright flash* to *dim steady* before he begins his crossover, for it is easier for me to fly on a steady light than a flashing one. Although this procedure came out of the death of pilots flying night formation on flashing lights, and is a required step before Two slides into position, I appreciate the thoughtfulness behind the action and the wisdom behind the rule.

Two moves slowly back eight feet, begins to move across behind the lead airplane. Half way to his new position, his airplane stops. Occasionally in a crossover an airplane will catch in the leader's jetwash and require a little nudge on stick and rudder to break again into smooth air, but Two is deliberately pausing. He is looking straight ahead into the tailpipe of Lead's engine.

It glows.

From a dark apple-red at the tip of it to a light luminous pink brighter than cockpit lights at their brightest, the tailpipe is alive and vibrant with light and heat. Tucked deep in the engine is the cherry-red turbine wheel, and Two is watching it spin.

Like the spokes of a quick-turning wagon wheel it spins, and every few seconds it strobes as he watches and appears to spin backwards. Two is saying to himself, again, "So that is how it works." He is not thinking of flying his airplane or of crossing over or of the seven miles of cold black air between his airplane and the hills. He is watching a beautiful machine at work, and he pauses in Lead's jetwash. I can see the red of the glow reflected in his windscreen, and on his white helmet.

Lead's voice comes softly in the tremendous quiet of the night. "Let's move it across, Two."

Two's helmet turns suddenly and I see his face clearly for a moment in the red glow of the tailpipe. Then his airplane slides quickly across into the space that I have been holding for him. The glow disappears from his windscreen.

In all the night formation missions, it is only when I fly as Two that I have the chance to see an engine soaked in its mystical light. The only other time that I can see a fire in the fire-driven turbine engines is at the moment of engine start, when I happen to be in one airplane parked behind another as the pilot presses his start switch upward. Then it is a weak twisting yellow flame that strains between the turbine blades for ten or fifteen seconds before it is gone and the tailpipe is dark again.

Newer airplanes, with afterburners, vaunt their flame on every takeoff, trailing a row of diamond shock waves in their blast that can be seen even in a noon sun. But the secret spinning furnace of a *Thunderstreak* engine at night is a sight that not many people have a chance to see, almost a holy sight. I keep it in my memory and think of it on other nights, on the ground, when there is not so much beauty in the sky.

The time always comes to go back down to the runway that we left waiting in the dark, and in the work of a night formation descent there is little chance for thoughts of the grace and the humble beauty of my airplane. I fly the steady light and try to make it smooth for Four on my wing and concentrate on keeping my airplane where it belongs. But even then, in the harder and more intense business of flying 20,000 pounds of fighter a few feet from another precisely the same, one part of my thought goes on thinking the most unrelated things and eagerly presenting for my consideration the most unlikely subjects.

I move it in just a bit more on Two and pull back just a bit of power because he is turning toward me and keep just a little more back stick pressure to hold my airplane up at its lower airspeed and should I let my daughter have a pair of Siamese kittens. Steady burns the green navigation light in my eyes and I press forward with my left thumb to make certain that the speed brake switch is all the way forward and add another second of power here, just a half-percent and pull it back right away and do they really climb curtains like someone told me? There will be absolutely no cats if they climb curtains. Little forward on the stick, little right bank to move it out one foot they certainly are handsome cats, though. Blue eyes. Fuel in a quick glance is 1,300 pounds, no problem; wonder how Four is doing out there on my wing, shouldn't be too difficult for him tonight, sometimes it's better to fly Four at night anyway, you have more reference points to line on. Wonder if Gene Ivan is taking the train to Zurich this weekend. Five months I've been in Europe and I haven't seen Zurich yet. Careful careful don't slide in too close, take it easy move it out a foot or two. Where's the runway? We should be coming up on the runway lights pretty soon now. Fly Two's wing here as he levels out. No problem. Just stay on the same plane with his wings. Add a bit more power . . . now peg it there. Hold what you have. If he moves an inch, correct for it right away. This is initial approach. Tuck it in. There is probably not a soul watching, at night. Doesn't matter. All we are is a bunch of navigation lights in the sky; move it in on Two's wing. Smooth now, smooth now for Four. Pardon the bounce, Four.

"Checkmate Lead is on the break." There goes Lead's light breaking away into the pattern. Been flying on that little bulb all night long, it seems. Move it in a little more on Two. Hold it in there just another three seconds.

"Checkmate Two's on the break." There we go. No more strain. Just the count to three. Almost over, Four. Few minutes and we can hang ourselves up to dry. Microphone button down.

"Checkmate Three's on the break." Don't care what kind of eyes they have, they don't live in my house if they climb curtains. Gear down. Flaps down. Lead's over the fence. Sometimes you can trick yourself into thinking that this is a pretty airplane. Button down. "Checkmate Three is turning base, three green, pressure and brakes." Check the brakes just to make sure. Yep. Brakes are good. This airplane has good brakes. Look out for the jetwash in this still air. Better tack on another three knots down final in case it's rough. There's the fence. Hold the nose up and let it land. Wonder if all runways have fences at the end. Can't think of any that don't. Little jetwash. We're down, little airplane. Nice job you did tonight. Drag chute handle out. Press the brakes once, lightly. Rollout is finished, a bit of brake to turn off the runway. Jettison the chute. Catch up with Lead and Two. Thanks for waiting, Lead. Pretty good flight. Pretty. If I have to be in the Air Force, wouldn't trade this job for any other they could offer. Canopy open. Air is warm. Nice to be down. I am wringing wet.

Over Luxembourg now, the distance-measuring drum unrolls smoothly, as though it was geared directly to the secondhand of the aircraft clock. Twenty-eight miles to Spangdahlem. My airplane grazes the top of the cloud and I begin to make the transition to instrument flying. There is another few minutes, perhaps, before I will be submerged in the cloud, but it is good to settle down to the routine of a crosscheck before it is really necessary. Airspeed is 265 indicated, altitude is 33,070 feet, turn needle is centered, vertical speed shows a hundred-foot-per-minute climb, the little airplane of the attitude indicator is very slightly nose-high on its horizon, heading indicator shows 086 degrees. The stars are still bright and unconcerned overhead. One nice thing about being a star is that you never have to worry about thunderstorms.

The radiocompass needle twists again to the right, in agony. It reminds me that I must not be certain of the smoothest flying ahead. Perhaps the forecaster was not completely wrong, after all. A distant flicker of lightning glitters in the southeast, and the thin needle shudders, a terrified finger pointing to the light. I remember the first time I heard of that characteristic of the radiocompass. I had been astonished. Of all the worst things for a navigation radio to do! Fly the needle as I am supposed to fly it and I wind up in the center of the biggest thunderstorm within a hundred miles. Who would design navigation equipment that worked like that? And who would buy it?

Any company that builds low-frequency radios, I learned, is the answer to the first question. The United States Air Force is the answer to the second. At least they had the honesty to tell me of this little eccentricity before they turned me loose on my first instrument crosscountry flight. When I need it most, in the worst weather, the last thing to count on is the radiocompass. It is better to fly time-and-distance than to follow the thin needle. I am glad that the newcomer, the TACAN, is not perturbed by the lightning.

Perhaps it is well that I do not have a wingman tonight. If I did near the edge of a storm, he would not have an easy time holding his position. That is one thing that I have never tried: thunderstorm formation flying.

The closest thing to that was in the air show that the squadron flew shortly before the recall, on Armed Forces Day. Somehow you can count on that day to have the roughest air of the year.

Every airplane in the squadron was scheduled to fly; a single giant formation of six four-ship diamonds of Air Guard F-84F's. I was surprised that there were so many people willing to drive bumper-to-bumper in the summer heat to watch, above the static displays, some old fighters flying.

Our airplanes are arranged in a long line in front of the bleachers erected for the day along the edge of the concrete parking ramp. I stand uncomfortably sunlit in front of my airplane at parade rest, watching the people waiting for the red flare that is the starting signal. If all those people go through the trouble of driving hot crowded miles to get here, why didn't they join the Air Force and fly the airplane themselves? Of every thousand that are here, 970 would have no difficulty flying this airplane. But still they would rather watch.

A little -pop-, and the brilliant scarlet flare streaks from the Very pistol of an adjutant standing near the visiting general in front of the reviewing stand. The flare soars up in a long smoky arc, and I move quickly, as much to hide myself from the gaze of the crowd as to strap myself into my airplane in unison with 23 other pilots, in 23 other airplanes. As I set my boots in the rudder pedal wells, I glance at the long straight line of airplanes and pilots to my left. There are none to my right, for I fly airplane number 24, as the slot man in the last diamond formation.

I snap my parachute buckles and reach back for the shoulder harness, studiously avoiding the massive gaze of the many people. If they are so interested, why didn't they learn to fly a long time ago?

The sweep secondhand of the aircraft clock is swinging up toward the 12, moving in accord with the secondhands of 23 other aircraft clocks. It is a sort of dance; a unison performance by all the pilots who make solo performances on their spare weekends. Battery *on*. Safety belt buckled, oxygen hoses attached. The secondhand touches the dot at the top of its dial. Starter switch to *start*. The concussion of my starter is a tiny part of the mass explosion of two dozen combustion starters. It is a rather loud sound, the engine start. The first rows of spectators shift backwards. But this is what they came to hear, the sound of these engines.

Behind us rises a solid bank of pure heat that ripples the trees on the horizon and slants up to lose itself in a pastel sky. The tachometer reaches 40 percent rpm, and I lift my white helmet from its comfortable resting place on the canopy bow, a foot from my head. Chin strap fastened (how many times have I heard of pilots losing their helmets when they bailed out with chin strap unfastened?), inverter selector to *normal*.

If the air were absolutely still today, I would even so be thoroughly buffeted by the jetwash of the 23 other airplanes ahead of me in flight. But the day is already a hot one, and the first airplane in the formation, the squadron commander's, will itself be stiffly jolted after takeoff into the boiling air of a July noon. In the air I will depend upon my flight leader to avoid the jetwash by flying beneath the level of the other airplanes, but there is no escaping the jetwash that will swirl across the runway as I take off on Baker Blue Three's wing, after all the other airplanes have rolled down the mile and a half of white concrete on this still day. After the squadron commander's takeoff, and because of the jetwash from his airplane and his wingman's, each successive takeoff roll will be just a little longer in the hot rough air that has been spun through rows of combustion chambers and stainless steel turbine blades. My takeoff roll will be the longest of all, and I will be working hard to stay properly on Three's wing in the turbulence of the airy whirlpools. But that is my job today, and I will do it.

To my left, far down the long line of airplanes, the squadron commander pushes his throttle ahead and begins to roll forward. "Falcon formation, check in," he calls on 24 radios, in 48 soft earphones, "Able Red Leader here."

"Able Red Two," his wingman calls.

"Three."

"Four."

A long succession of filtered voices and microphone buttons pressed. Throttle comes forward in cockpit after cockpit, fighter after fighter pivots to the left and swings to follow the polished airplane of the squadron commander. My flight leader takes his turn. "Baker Blue Leader," he calls, rolling forward. His name is Cal Whipple.

"Two." Gene Ivan.

"Three." Allen Dexter.

[83]

I press my microphone button, at last. "Four." And it is quiet. There is no one left after the slot man of the sixth flight.

The long line of airplanes rolls briskly along the taxiway to runway three zero, and the first airplane taxies well down the runway to leave room for his multitude of wingmen. The great formation moves quickly to fill the space behind him, for there is no time allowed for unnecessary taxi time. Twenty-four airplanes on the runway at once, a rare sight. I press my microphone button as I roll to a stop in position by Baker Blue Three's wing, and have a private little talk with the squadron commander. "Baker Blue Four is in."

When he hears from me, the man in the polished airplane, with the little cloth oak leaves on the shoulders of his flight suit, pushes his throttle forward and calls, "Falcon formation, run it up."

It is not really necessary for all 24 airplanes to turn their engines up to 100 percent rpm at the same moment, but it does make an impressive noise, and that is what the people in the stands would like to hear this day. Two dozen throttles go full forward against their stops.

Even with canopy locked and a helmet and earphones about my head, the roar is loud. The sky darkens a little and through the massive thunder that shakes the wooden bleachers, the people watch a great cloud of exhaust smoke rise from the end of the runway, above the shining pickets that are the tall swept stabilizers of Falcon formation. I jolt and rock on my wheels in the blast from the other airplanes, and notice that, as I expected, my engine is not turning up its normal 100 percent. For just a second it did, but as the heat and pressured roar of the other airplanes swept back to cover my air intake, the engine speed fell off to a little less than 98 percent rpm. That is a good indicator

[84]

that the air outside my small conditioned cockpit is warm.

"Able Red Leader is rolling." The two forwardmost pickets separate and pull slowly away from the forest of pickets, and Falcon formation comes to life. Five seconds by the sweep secondhand and Able Red Three is rolling to follow, Four at his wing.

I sit high in my cockpit and watch, far ahead, the first of the formation lift from the runway.

The first airplanes break from the ground as if weary of it and glad to be back home in the air. Their exhaust trails are dark as I look down the length of them, and I wonder with a smile if I will have to go on instruments through the smoke of the other airplanes by the time I begin to roll with Baker Blue Three.

Two by two by two they roll. Eight; ten; twelve . . . I wait, watching my rpm down to 97 percent now at full throttle, hoping that I can stay with Three on the roll and break ground with him as I should. We have the same problem, so there should be no difficulty other than a very long takeoff roll.

I look over toward Three, ready to nod OK at him. He is watching the other airplanes take off, and does not look back. He is watching them go . . . sixteen; eighteen; twenty . . .

The runway is nearly empty in front of us, under a low cloud of grey smoke. The overrun barrier at the other end of the concrete is not even visible in the swirl of heat. But except for a little bit of sudden wing-rocking, the earlier flights get away from the ground without difficulty, though they clear the barrier by a narrower and narrower margin.

. . . twenty-two. Three looks back to me at last and I nod my OK. Baker Blue Lead and Two are five seconds down the concrete when Three touches his helmet back to the red ejection seat headrest, nods sharply forward, and we become the last of Falcon formation to release brakes. Left rudder, right rudder. I can feel the turbulence over the runway on my stabilizer, through the rudder pedals. It is taking a long time to gain airspeed and I am glad that we have the full length of the runway for our takeoff roll. Three rocks up and down slightly as his airplane moves heavily over the ripples in the concrete. I follow as if I were a shining aluminum shadow in three dimensions, bouncing when he bounces, sweeping ahead with him, slowly gaining airspeed. Blue Lead and Two must be lifting off by now, though I do not move my eyes from Three to check. They have either lifted off by now or they are in the barrier. It is at this moment one of the longest takeoff rolls I have seen in the F-84F, passing the 7,500-foot mark. The weight of Three's airplane just now finishes the change from wheels to swept wings, and we ease together into the air. A highly improbable bit of physics, this trusting 12 tons to thin air; but it has worked before and it should today.

Three is looking ahead and for once I am glad that I must watch his airplane so closely. The barrier is reaching to snag our wheels, and it is only a hundred feet away. Three climbs suddenly away from the ground and I follow, pulling harder on the control stick than I should have to, forcing my airplane to climb before it is ready to fly.

The helmet in the cockpit a few feet away nods once, sharply, and without looking, I reach forward and move the landing gear lever to *up*. There is the flash of the barrier going beneath us, in the same second that I touched the gear handle. We had ten feet to spare. It is good, I think, that I was not number twenty-six in this formation.

The landing gear tucks itself quickly up and out of the way, and the background behind Three changes from one of smooth concrete to rough blurred brush-covered ground; we are very definitely committed to fly. The turbulence, surprisingly enough, was only a passing shock, for our take-off is longer and lower than any other, and we fly beneath the heaviest whirlpools in the air.

A low and gentle turn to the right to join on Blue Leader and Two as quickly as possible. But the turn is not my worry, for I am just a sandbagger, loafing along on Three's wing while he does all the juggling and angling and cutting off to make a smooth joinup. The worry of the long takeoff roll is left behind with the barrier, and now, takeoff accomplished, I feel as if I sat relaxed in the softest armchair in the pilots' lounge.

The familiar routine of a formation flight settles down upon me; I can hold it a little loose here over the trees and away from the crowd. There will be plenty of work ahead to fly the slot during the passes over the base.

There in the corner of my eye drifts Blue Leader and Two, closing nicely above and back to Three's left wing. Around them are the silver flashes and silhouettes that make the mass of swept metal called Falcon formation, juggling itself into the positions drawn out on green blackboards still chalked and standing in the briefing room. The wrinkles in the monster formation have been worked out in a practice flight, and the practice is paying off now as the finger-fours form into diamonds and the diamonds form into vees and the vees become the invincible juggernaut of Falcon formation.

I slide across into the slot between Two and Three, directly behind Baker Blue Leader, and move my airplane forward until Lead's tailpipe is a gaping black hole ten feet ahead of my windscreen and I can feel the buffet of his jetwash in my rudder pedals. Now I forget about Three and

fly a close trail formation on Lead, touching the control
stick back every once in a while to keep the buffet on the
rudder pedals.

"Falcon formation, go channel nine."

Blue Lead yaws his airplane slightly back and forth, and
with the other five diamonds in the sky, the four-ship
diamond that is Baker Blue flight spreads itself for a moment while its pilots click their radio channel selectors to
9 and make the required cockpit check after takeoff.

I push the switches aft of the throttle quadrant, and the
drop tanks under my wings begin feeding their fuel to the
main fuselage tank and to the engine. Oxygen pressure is
70 psi, the blinker blinks as I breathe, engine instruments
are in the green. I leave the engine screens extended, the
parachute lanyard hooked to the ripcord handle. My airplane is ready for its airshow.

In this formation there are probably some airplanes that
are not operating just as they should, but unless the difficulties are serious ones, the pilots keep their troubles to
themselves and call the cockpit check OK. Today it would
be too embarrassing to return to the field and shoot a
forced landing pattern on the high stage before an audience
so large.

"Baker Blue Lead is good."

"Two."

"Three."

I press the button. "Four."

Normally the check would have been a longer one, with
each pilot calling his oxygen condition and quantity and
whether or not his drop tanks were feeding properly, but
with so many airplanes aloft the check alone would take
minutes. It was agreed in the briefing room to make the
check as usual, but to reply only with flight call sign.

Six lead airplanes rock their wings after my call and the six diamonds close again to show formation. I do not often have the chance to fly as slot man in diamond, and I tuck my airplane in close under Lead's tailpipe to make it look from the ground as if I had flown there all my life. The way to tell if a slot man has been flying his position well is to look at his vertical stabilizer as he lands. The blacker his stabilizer and rudder with Lead's exhaust, the better the formation he has been flying.

I move up for a moment into the position that I will hold during our passes across the base. When I feel that it is correct, the black gaping hole of Lead's tailpipe is a shimmering inky disc six feet forward of my windscreen and a foot above the level of my canopy. My vertical stabilizer is solid in his jetwash, and I ease the weight of my boots from the rudder pedals to avoid the uncomfortable vibration in them. If it were possible to move my boots completely off the pedals, I would, but the slanting tunnels that lead down to them offer no resting-place, and I must live with the vibration that means that the stabilizer is blackening in burnt JP-4. I can hear it, a dull heavy constant rumble of twisted forced air beating against the rudder. The airplane does not fly easily in this, and it is not enjoyable to fly with the tail, like a great dorsal fin, forced into the stream of heat from Baker Blue Lead's turbine. But that is the position that I must fly to make Baker Blue flight a close and perfect diamond, and the people who will watch are not interested in my problems. I move the throttle back an inch and ahead again, touch the control stick forward, sliding away and down into a looser, easier formation.

Two and Three are using the time that Falcon formation spends in its wide turn to check their own positions. The air is rough, and their airplanes shudder and jolt as they move in to overlap their wings behind Lead's. To fly a tight formation, they must close on the leader until their wings are fitted in the violent wake of Lead's wing. Although that air is not so rough as the heat that blasts my rudder, it is more difficult to fly, for it is an unbalanced force, and a changing one. At 350 knots the air is as solid as sheet steel, and I can see the ailerons near their wingtips move quickly up and down as they fight to hold smoothly in formation. During normal formation flying, their wings would be just outside the river of air washing back from their leader's wing, and they could fly that position for a long time with the normal working and coaxing and correcting. But this is a show, and for a show we work.

Two and Three are apparently satisfied that they will be able to hold a good position for the passes across the base, for they slide out into normal formation almost simultaneously. Still they watch nothing but Baker Blue Lead, and still they bounce and jar in the rough air. Every few seconds the flight slams across an invisible whirlwind twisting up from a plowed field, and the impact of it is a solid thing that blurs my vision for an instant and makes me grateful for my shoulder harness.

This is summer on an air base: not blazing sun and crowded pool and melting ice cream, but the jarring slam of rough air when I want to tuck my airplane into close formation.

The wide circle is completed, and Falcon formation begins to descend to its 500-foot flyby altitude.

"Close it up, Falcon," comes the voice of the man who is Able Red Leader. We close it up, and I lift my airplane to push the rudder again into Lead's tumbling jetwash. I glance at my altimeter when the formation is level and three miles from the crowd by the runway. One quick glance: 400 feet above the ground. The leading vee of diamonds is at 500 feet and we are stacked 100 feet beneath it. As a slot man, altitude is none of my business, but I am curious.

Now, in these last three miles to the base, we are being watched by the American people. They are interested in knowing just how well the part-time Air Force can fly its airplanes.

The diamonds of Falcon formation are hard and glittering in the sun, and even from the center of Baker Blue flight the formation looks close and good. I think again the old axiom of bouncing in the same air with the leader, and I am not alone with the thought. Two and Three have placed their wings unnervingly close to Lead's smooth fuselage, and we take the ridges of the air as a close formation of bobsleds would take the ridges of hardpacked snow. Slam. Four helmets jerk, four sets of stiff wings flex the slightest bit. My rudder is full in Lead's jetwash and the pedals are chattering heavily. This rumble of hard jetwash must be loud even to the people standing by the bleachers on the flight line. Hold it smooth. Hold it steady. Hold it close.

But the people on the concrete do not even begin to hear the rumble that makes my rudder pedals dance. They see from the north a little cloud of grey smoke on the horizon. It stretches to become a quiver of grey arrows in flight, shot at once from a single bow. There is no sound.

The arrows grow, and the people on the ground talk to each other in the quiet air as they watch. The arrowheads slice the air at 400 knots, but from the ground they seem to be suspended in cold clear honey.

Then, as the silent flight reaches the end of the runway a quarter-mile from the bleachers and even the visiting general is smiling to himself behind his issue sunglasses, the honey becomes only air and the 400 knots is the ground-shaking blast of 24 sudden detonations of high explosive. The people wince happily in the burst of sound and watch the diamonds whip together through the sky in unyielding immovable grace. In that moment the people on the ground are led to believe that Air Guard airplanes are not left to rust unused in the sun, and this is what we are trying to tell them.

In one fading dopplered roar we flick past the stands and are to the people a line of dwindling dots, pulling two dozen streamers of tenuous grey as we go. Our sound is gone as quickly as it came, and the ground is quiet again.

But still, after we pass the crowd, we fly formation. Baker Blue flight and Falcon formation are just as present about me as they have been all morning. The brief roar that swept the people is to me unchanged and constant. The only change in Falcon formation after it crosses the field is that the diamonds loosen a few feet out and back, and the bobsleds take the ridges a tenth-second apart rather than in the same instant.

During the turn to the second pass across the base, I slide with Baker Blue Lead to form a new pattern in which our diamond is the corner of a giant block of airplanes. Regardless of the position that we fly, the rough sky beats at our airplanes and the jetwash thunders over my vertical stabilizer. I think of the landing that is ahead, hoping that a light breeze has begun across the runway, to clear the jet-wash out of the way by the time my airplane slides down final approach to land.

Maybe they don't want to be pilots.

Where did that come from? Of course they want to be pilots. Yet they watch from the ground instead of flying wing in Baker Blue flight. The only reason that they are not flying today instead of watching is that they do not know what they are missing. What better work is there than flying airplanes? If flying was the full-time employment of an Air Force pilot, I would have become a career officer when the chance was offered me.

We force our airplanes close again, fly the second pass, re-form into a final design and bring it through the rocky air above the field. Then, from a huge circle out of sight of the runway, flight after flight separates from the formation, diamonds changing to echelon right, and the echelons fly a long straight approach across the hard uneven air into the landing pattern.

It is work, it is uncomfortable. The needle that measures G has been knocked to the number 4. But in the moments that the people watch this part of their standby Air Force, and were glad for it, the flight was worthwhile. Able Red Leader has completed another little part of his job.

That was months ago. These days, in Europe, our formation is not for show but for the business of fighting. A four-ship flight is loose and comfortable when it is not being watched, and the pilots merely concentrate on their position, rather than devote their every thought and smallest action to show flying. At altitude we wait for the left-right yaw of the lead airplane, and spread out even more, into tactical formation. Three and Four climb together a thousand feet above Lead and Two; each wingman sliding to a loose angled trailing position from which he can watch the sky around as well as the airplane that he protects. In tactical formation and the practice of air combat, responsibility is sharply defined: wingman clears leader, high element clears low element, leaders look for targets.

Flying at the contrail altitudes, this is easy. Any con other than our own four are bogies. During a war, when they are identified, they become either bogies to be watched or bandits to be judged and occasionally, attacked. "Occasionally" because our airplane was not designed to engage enemy fighters at altitude and destroy them. That is the job of the F-104's and the Canadian Mark Sixes and the French *Mystères*. Our *Thunderstreak* is an air-to-ground attack airplane built to carry bombs and rockets and napalm against the enemy as he moves on the earth. We attack enemy airplanes only when they are easy targets: the transports and the low-speed bombers and the propeller-driven fighters. It is not fair and not sporting to attack only a weaker enemy, but we are not a match for the latest enemy airplanes built specifically to engage other fighters.

But we practice air combat against the day when we are engaged over our target by enemy fighters. If hours of practice suffice only to allow us a successful escape from a more powerful fighter, they will have been worthwhile. And the practice is interesting.

There they are. Two '84F's at ten o'clock low, in a long circling climb into the contrail level, coming up like goldfish to food on the surface. At 30,000 feet the bogie lead element begins to pull a con. The high element is nowhere in sight.

I am Dynamite Four, and I watch them from my high perch. It is slow motion. Turns at altitude are wide and gentle, for too much bank and G will stall the airplane in the thin air and I will lose my most precious commodity: airspeed. Airspeed is golden in combat. There are books filled with rules, but one of the most important is Keep Your Mach Up. With speed I can outmaneuver the enemy.

I can dive upon him from above, track him for a moment in my gunsight, fire, pull up and away, prepare another attack. Without airspeed I cannot even climb, and drift at altitude like a helpless duck in a pond.

I call the bogies to Three, my element leader, and look around for the others. After the first enemy airplanes are seen, it is the leader's responsibility to watch them and plan an attack. I look out for other airplanes and keep my leader clear. When I am a wingman, it is not my job to shoot down enemy airplanes. It is my job to protect the man who is doing the shooting. I turn with Three, shifting back and forth across his tail, watching, watching.

And there they are. From above the con level, from five o'clock high, come a pair of swept dots. Turning in on our tail. I press the microphone button. "Dynamite Three, bogies at five high."

Three continues his turn to cover Dynamite Lead during his attack on the bogie lead element in their climb. The decoys. "Watch 'em," he calls.

I watch, twisted in my seat with the top of my helmet touching the canopy as I look. The two are counting on surprise, and are only this moment, with plenty of airspeed, beginning to pull cons. I wait for them, watching them close on us, begin to track us. They are F-84's. We can outfly them. They don't have a chance.

"Dynamite Three, break right!" For once the wingman orders the leader, and Three twists into a steep bank and pulls all the backpressure that he can without stalling the airflow over his wings. I follow, seeking to stay on the inside of his turn, and watching the attackers. They are going too fast to follow our turn, and they begin to overshoot and slide to the outside of it. They are not unwise, though, for immediately they pull back up, converting their airspeed into altitude for another pass. But they have lost the surprise that they had counted on, and with full throttle we are gaining airspeed. The fight is on.

A fight in the air proceeds like the scurrying of minnows about a falling crumb of bread. It starts at high altitudes, crossing and recrossing the sky with bands of grey contrail, and slowly moves lower and lower. Every turn means a little more altitude lost. Lower altitudes mean that airplanes can turn more tightly, gain speed more quickly, pull more G before they stall. Around and around the fight goes, through the tactics and the language of air combat: scissors, defensive splits, yo-yos and "Break right, Three!"

I do not even squeeze my trigger. I watch for other airplanes, and after Three rivets his attention on one enemy airplane, I am the only eyes in the element that watch for danger. Three is totally absorbed in his attack, depending on me to clear him of enemy planes. If I wanted to kill him in combat, I would simply stop looking around.

In air combat more than at any other time, I am the thinking brain for a living machine. There is no time to keep my head in the cockpit or to watch gages or to look for switches. I move the control stick and the throttle and the rudder pedals unconsciously. I want to be *there,* and I am there. The ground does not even exist until the last minutes of a fight that was allowed to get too low. I fly and fight in a block of space. The ideal game of three-dimension chess, across which moves are made with reckless abandon.

In two-ship combat there is only one factor to consider: the enemy airplane. I seek only to stay on his tail, to track him with the pipper in the gunsight and pull the trigger that takes closeups of his tailpipe. If he should be on my tail, there are no holds barred. I do everything that I can to keep him from tracking me in his gunsight, and to begin to track him. I can do maneuvers in air combat that I could never repeat if I tried.

I saw an airplane tumble once, end over end. For one shocked moment the fighter was actually moving backwards and smoke was streaming from both ends of the airplane. Later on, on the ground, we deduced that the pilot had forced his aircraft into a wild variation of a snap roll, which is simply not done in heavy fighter airplanes. But the maneuver certainly got the enemy off his tail.

As more airplanes enter the fight, it becomes complicated. I must consider that this airplane is friend and that airplane is enemy, and that I must watch my rolls to the left because there are two airplanes in a fight there and I would fly right through the middle of them. Midair collisions are rare, but they are always a possibility when one applies too much abandon in many-ship air combat flights.

John Larkin was hit in the air by a *Sabre* that saw him too late to turn. "I didn't know what had happened," he told me. "But my airplane was tumbling and it didn't take long to figure that I had been hit. I pulled the seat handle and squeezed the trigger and the next thing I remember, I was in the middle of a little cloud of airplane pieces, just separating from the seat.

"I was at a pretty good altitude, about thirty-five thousand, so I free-fell down to where I could begin to see color on the ground. Just when I reached for my ripcord, the automatic release pulled it for me and I had a good chute. I watched the tail of my airplane spin down by me and saw it crash in the hills. A couple of minutes later I was down myself and thinking about all the paperwork I was going to have to fill out."

There had been a great amount of paperwork, and the thought of it makes me doubly careful when I fly air combat, even today. In a war, without the paperwork, I will be a little more free in my fighting.

When it spirals down to altitudes where dodging hills enters the tactic, a fight is broken off by mutual consent, as boxers hold their fists when an opponent is in the ropes. In the real war, of course, it goes on down to the ground, and I pick up all the pointers I can on methods to scrape an enemy into a hillside. It could all be important someday.

The wide luminous needle of the TACAN swings serenely as I pass over Spangdahlem at 2218, and one more leg of the flight is complete.

As if it recognized that Spangdahlem is a checkpoint and time for things to be happening, the thick dark cloud puts an end to its toying and abruptly lifts to swallow my airplane in blackness. For a second it is uncomfortable, and I sit tall in my seat to see over the top of the cloud. But the second quickly passes and I am on instruments.

For just a moment, though, I look up through the top of my canopy. Above, the last bright star fades and the sky above is as dark and faceless as it is about me. The stars are gone, and I am indeed on instruments.

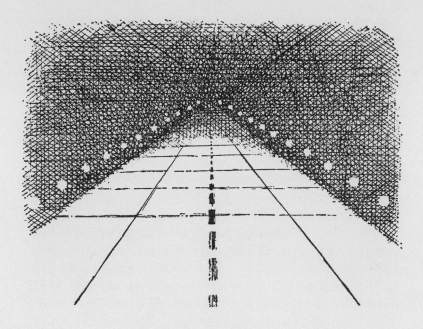

CHAPTER FOUR

"Rhein Control, Air Force Jet Two Niner Four Zero Five, Spangdahlem, over." From my capricious radio I do not know whether or not to expect an answer. The "over," which I rarely use, is a wistful sort of hope. I am doubtful.

"Jet Four Zero Five, Rhein Control, go ahead."

Someday I will give up trying to predict the performance of a UHF radio. "Roger, Rhein, Zero Five was Spangdahlem at two niner, flight level three three zero assigned instrument flight rules, Wiesbaden at three seven, Phalsbourg next. Latest weather at Chaumont Air Base, please." A long pause of faint flowing static. My thumb is beginning to be heavy on the microphone button.

"Roger your position, Zero Five. Latest Chaumont weather is one thousand overcast, visibility five miles in rain, winds from the west at one zero knots."

"Thank you, Rhein. How about the Phalsbourg weather?" The static is suddenly louder and there is a light blue glow across the windscreen. St. Elmo's fire. Harmless and pretty to watch, but it turns low-frequency radio navigation into a patchwork of guesses and estimates. The radiocompass needle is wobbling in an aimless arc. It is good to have a TACAN set.

"Zero Five, Phalsbourg weather is garbled on our machine. Strasbourg is calling eight hundred overcast, visibility one-half mile in heavy rain showers, winds variable two zero gusting three zero knots, isolated thunderstorms all quadrants." Strasbourg is to the left of course, but I could catch the edge of their thunderstorms. Too bad that Phalsbourg is out. Always seems to happen when you need it most.

"What is the last weather you had from Phalsbourg, Rhein?" A garbled teletype weather report is really garbled. It is either a meaningless mass of consonants or a black jumble where one weather sequence has been typed on top of another.

"Latest we have, sir, is two hours old. They were calling five hundred overcast, visibility one-quarter mile in . . ." he pauses, and his thumb comes off the microphone button. It comes on again ". . . hail—that might be a misprint—scattered thunderstorms all quadrants." Quarter-mile visibility in hail. I have heard that nocturnal thunderstorms can be violent, but this is the first time that I have heard the direct report as I fly on instruments in the weather. But the sequence is two hours old, and the storms are isolated. It is rare for storms to hold their violence for a long time, and I can get a radar vector from a ground station around active storm cells.

"Thank you, Rhein." The air is very smooth in the stratus, and it is not difficult to hold the new heading at 093 degrees. But I am beginning to think that perhaps my detour did not take me far enough around the severe weather.

I am well established in the routine of the crosscheck now, and occasionally look forward to the liquid blue fire on the windscreen. It is a brilliant cobalt, glowing with an inner light that is somehow startling to see at high altitude. And it is liquid as water is liquid; it twists across the glass in little rivulets of blue rain against the black of the night weather. The light of it, mingling with the red of the cockpit lights, turns the instrument panel into a surrealist's impression of a panel, in heavy oil paint. In the steady red and flickering blue of the electrical fire on the glass, the only difference between my needles and the painter's is that a few of mine are moving.

Turn back.

The air is smooth. The needles, except for the wobbling radiocompass needle and the rolling numbered drums of the distance-measuring equipment, move only the smallest fractions of inches as I make the gentle corrections to stay at 33,000 feet. The airplane is flying well and the UHF is back in action.

There are storms ahead, and this airplane is very small.

My crosscheck goes so smoothly that I do not have to hurry to include a look at the fuel flow and quantity gages, the pale green oxygen blinker blinking coolly at me as I breathe, the utility and flight control system pressure gages, the voltmeter, the loadmeter, the tailpipe temperature. They are all my friends, and they are all in the green.

I will not live through the storms.

What is this? Fear? The little half-noticed voices that flit through my thought like scurrying fireflies might warrant the name of fear, but only if I stretch the definition until it applies to the thoughts that scurry before I begin to walk across a busy highway. If I reacted to the half-thoughts, I would have quit flying before I made my first flight in the light propeller-driven trainer that first lifted me away from a runway.

The Florida sky is a gay blue one, puffing with the high cumulus that prevails in southern summers. The metal of my primary trainer is hot in the sun, but before my first flight in the United States Air Force, I am not concerned with heat.

The man who settles himself in the rear cockpit of the airplane is not a big man, but he has the quiet confidence of one who has all power and knows all things.

"Start the engine and let's get out of here," are the first words that I hear in an airplane from a flight instructor.

I am not so confident as he, but I move the levers and switches that I have studied in the handbook and call, "Clear!" as I know I should. Then I touch the starter switch to *start,* and feel for the first time that strange instant awareness of my ability to do everything that I should. And I begin to learn.

I discover, as the months pass, that the only time that I am afraid in an airplane is when I do not know what must be done next.

The engine stops on takeoff. Whistling beneath my airplane is a swamp of broken trees and hanging spanish moss and alligators and water moccasins and no dry ground for wheel to roll upon. At one time I would have been afraid, for at one time I did not know what to do about the engine failure and the swamp and the alligators. I would have had time to think, So this is how I will die, before I hit the trees and my airplane twisted and somersaulted and sank in the dark green water.

But by the time that I am able to fly the airplane by myself, I know. Instead of dying, I lower the nose, change fuel tanks, check the fuel boost pumps *on* and the mixture *rich,* retract the landing gear and wing flaps, pump the throttle, aim the airplane so that the fuselage and cockpit will go between the tree stumps, pull the yellow handle that jettisons the canopy, lock the shoulder harness, turn the magneto and battery switches off, and concentrate on making a smooth landing on the dark water. I trust the shoulder harness and I trust my skill and I forget about the alligators. In two hours I am flying another airplane over the same swamp.

I learn that it is what I do not know that I fear, and I strive, outwardly from pride, inwardly from the knowledge that the unknown is what will finally kill me, to know all there is to be known about my airplane. I will never die.

My best friend is the pilot's handbook, a different book for each type of airplane that I fly. Technical Order 1F-84F-1 describes my airplane; every switch and knob of it. It gives the normal operating procedures, and on red-bordered pages, the emergency procedures for practically any critical situation that can arise while I sit in the cockpit. The pilot's handbook tells me what the airplane feels like to fly, what it will do and what it will not do, what to expect from it as it goes through the speed of sound, procedures to follow if I suddenly find myself in an airplane that has been pushed too far and has begun to spin. It has detailed charts of my airplane's performance to tell just how many miles it will fly, how quickly it will fly them, and how much fuel it will need.

I study the flight handbook as a divinity student studies the Bible. And as he goes back time and again to Psalms, so I go back time and again to the red-bordered pages of Section III. Engine fire on takeoff; after takeoff; at altitude. Loss of oil pressure. Severe engine vibration. Smoke in the cockpit. Loss of hydraulic pressure. Electrical failure. This procedure is the best to be done, this one is not recommended.

In cadet days, I studied the emergency procedures in class and in spare time and shouted them as I ran to and from my barracks. When I know the words of the red-bordered pages well enough to shout them word for word as I run down a long sidewalk lined with critical upperclass cadets, it can be said I know them well.

The shined black shoe touches the sidewalk. Run. "GLIDE NINETY KNOTS CHANGE FUEL TANKS BOOST PUMPS ON CHECK FUEL PRESSURE MIXTURE RICH PROP FULL INCREASE GEAR UP FLAPS UP CANOPY OPEN . . ." I know the forced landing procedures for that first trainer as well today as I knew them then. And I was not afraid of that first airplane.

But not every emergency can be put in a book, not even in a pilot's handbook. The marginal situations, such as planning a flight to an airport that I know is buried in solid weather to its minimums, such as losing sight of my leader in a formation letdown through the weather, such as continuing a flight into an area of thunderstorms, is left to a thing called pilot judgment. It is up to me in those cases. Bring all of my experience and knowledge of my airplane into play, evaluate the variables: fuel, weather, other aircraft flying with me, condition of the runway, importance of the mission—against the severity of the storms. Then, like a smooth-humming computer, I come up with one plan of action and follow it. Cancel the flight until I get more rest. Make a full circle in the weather and make my own let-down after my leader has made his. Continue toward the storms. Turn back.

When I make the judgment I follow it without fear, for it is what I have decided is the best course of action. Any other course would be a risky one. Only in the insecure hours before I touch the starter switch can I see causes for fear; when I do not take the effort to be alert.

On the ground, if I concentrated, I could be afraid, in a detached, theoretical sort of way. But so far I have not met the pilot who concentrated on it.

I like to fly airplanes, so I learn about them and I fly them. I think of my job in the same light that a bridge builder on the high steel thinks of his: it has its dangers, but it is still a good way to make a living. The danger is an interesting factor, for I do not know if my next flight will be an uneventful one or not. Every once in a long while I am called to step on the stage, under the spotlight, and cope with an unusual situation, or, at longer intervals, an emergency.

Unusual situations come in all sizes, from false alarms to full-fledged emergencies that involve my continued existence as a living member of a fighter squadron.

I lower my landing gear on the turn to final approach. The little green lights that indicate wheels locked in the down position are dark longer than they should be. The right main gear locks down, showing its light. The left main locks down. But the nosewheel light is dark. I wait a moment and sigh. The nosewheel is a bother, but not in the least is it an emergency. As soon as I see that it is not going to lock down, the cautious part of me thinks of the very worst that this could mean. It could mean at worst that the nosegear is still locked up in its wheel well; that I will not be able to lower it; that I will have to land on only two wheels.

There is no danger (oh, once long ago an '84 cartwheeled during a nosegear-up landing and the pilot was killed), even if that very worst thing happens. If the normal gear lowering system does not work after I try it a few times again; if the emergency gear lowering system, which blows the nosegear down with a high-pressure charge of compressed air, fails; if I cannot shake the wheel loose by bouncing the main gear against the runway . . . if all these fail, I still have no cause for concern (unless the airplane cartwheels). Fuel permitting, I will circle the field for a few minutes and the fire trucks will lay a long strip of white foam down the runway, a place for my airplane's unwheeled nose to slide. And I will land.

Final approach is the same final approach that it has always been. The fence pulls by beneath the wheels as it always does, except that now it pulls beneath two landing gear instead of three, and with a gear warning horn loud in the cockpit and the red warning light brilliant in the clear plastic handle and the third green light dark and the word from the control tower is that the nosewheel still looks as if it is up and locked.

The biggest difference in the final approach is in the eye of the observer, and observers are many. When the square red fire trucks grind to the runway with their red beacons flashing, the line crews and returning pilots climb to stand on the swept silver wings of parked airplanes and watch to see what will happen. (Look at that, Johnny, turning final with no nosewheel. Heard about an eighty-four that cartwheeled on the runway trying this same trick. Good luck, whoever you are, don't forget to hold the nose off as long as you can.) It is interesting to them, and mildly annoying to me, for it is like being pushed on stage without having anything to perform. No flames, no eerie silence of a frozen engine, a practically nonexistent threat of spectacular destruction, no particular skill on display.

I simply land, and the twin plumes of blue rubber-smoke pout back from the main wheels as they touch the hard concrete. I slow through 100 knots on the landing roll, touching right rudder to put the narrow strip of foam between the wheels. Then, slowly and gently, the unwheeled nose of the airplane comes down.

At that moment before the metal of the nose touches the runway and I tilt unnaturally forward in my cockpit and the only sight in the windscreen is the fast-blurred strip of white foam, I am suddenly afraid. This is where my control ends and chance takes over. A gust of wind against the high rudder and I will surely cartwheel in a flying swirling cloud of brilliant orange flame and twisted metal; the airplane will tumble and I will be caught beneath it; the hot engine will explode when the cold foam sprays up the intake. The ground is hard and it is moving very fast and it is very close.

Throttle *off*, and the nose settles into the foam.

White. Instant white and the world outside is cut away and metal screams against concrete loudly and painfully and I grit my teeth and squint my eyes behind the visor and know in a surprised shock that my airplane is being hurt and she doesn't deserve to be hurt and she is good and faithful and she is taking the force of a 90-knot slab of concrete and I can do nothing to ease her pain and I am not cartwheeling and the scream will never end and I must have slid a thousand feet and I am still slammed hard forward

[107]

into the shoulder harness and the world is white because the canopy is sprayed with foam and get that canopy open now, while I'm still sliding.

The foam-covered sheet of plexiglass lifts as I pull the unlock lever, as smoothly as if nothing was the least unusual and there is the world again, blue sky and white runway sliding to a stop and grass at the side of the concrete and visor up and oxygen mask unsnapped and it is very quiet. The air is fresh and smooth and green and I am alive. Battery *off* and fuel *off*. As quiet as I have ever heard. My airplane is hurt and I love her very much. She didn't somersault or cartwheel or flip on her back to burn and I owe my life to her.

The advancing roar of firetruck engines and soon we'll be surrounded by the square monsters and by talking people and Say, why couldn't you get the nosewheel down and That landing was a pretty good one boy and You should have seen the foam spray when your nose hit. But before the people come, I sit quietly in the cockpit for a second that seems a long time and tell my airplane that I love her and that I will not forget that she did not trap me beneath her or explode on the runway and that she took the pain while I walk away without a scratch and that a secret that I will keep between us is that I love her more than I would tell to anyone who asks.

I will someday tell that secret to another pilot, when he and I happen to be walking back from a night formation flight and the breeze is cool and the stars are as bright as they can get when you walk on the ground. I will say in the quiet, "Our airplane is a pretty good airplane." He will be quiet a second longer than he should be quiet and he will say, "It is." He will know what I have said. He will know that I love our airplane not because she is like a living thing, but because she truly is a living thing and so very many people think that she is just a block of aluminum and glass and bolts and wire. But I know and my friend will know and that is all that must be said.

Though it had its moment of fear and though it opened the door of understanding a little wider, the nosegear failure is an incident, not an emergency. I have had a few incidents in the hours that I have spent in the little cockpit, but so far I have never experienced a real emergency or been forced to make the decision to pull the yellow ejection seat handles, squeeze the red trigger, and say a quick farewell to a dying airplane. Yet that sort of thing is what the newspapers would have me believe happens every day in the Air Force.

At first, I was ready for it. When the engine sounded rough during those first hours alone, I thought of the ejection seat. When a tailpipe overheat light came on for the first time in my career, I thought of the ejection seat. When I was nearly out of fuel and lost in the weather, I thought of it. But the part of my mind that is concerned with caution can cry wolf only so many times before I see through its little game and realize that I could easily fly through my entire career without being called upon to blast away from an airplane into a cold sky. But still it is good to know that a 37-millimeter cannon shell is waiting just aft of the seat, waiting for the moment that I squeeze the trigger.

If I ever collide with another airplane in the air, the seat is waiting to throw me clear. If I lose all hydraulic pressure to the flight controls, it is waiting. If I am spinning and have not begun to recover as the ground nears, the seat is waiting. It is an advantage that conventional aircraft and transport pilots do not have, and I feel a little sorry for them at their dangerous job.

Even without passengers to think about, if they are hit in the air by another airplane, transport pilots do not have a chance to crawl back to the trap door on the floor of the flight deck and bail out. They can only sit in their seats and fight the useless controls of a wing that is not there and spin down until their airplane stops against the ground.

But not the single-engine pilot. Climbing or diving or inverted or spinning or coming to pieces, his airplane is rarely the place that he dies. There is a narrow margin near the ground where even the ejection seat is a game of chance, and I am in that margin for five seconds after the end of the runway has passed beneath me. After that five seconds I have accelerated to a speed that allows a climb to a safe ejection altitude; before that five seconds I can put my airplane back down on the runway and engage the nylon webbing and steel cable of the overrun barrier. When I engage that barrier, even at 150 knots, I drag a steel cable and the cable drags a long length of anchor chain and no airplane in the world can run on forever with tons of massive chain trailing behind it. The five seconds are the critical ones. Even before I retract the flaps after takeoff, I can eject if the engine explodes. And no engine explodes without warning.

Flying is safe, and flying a single-engine fighter plane is the safest of all flying. I would much rather fly from one place to another than drive it in that incredibly dangerous thing called an automobile. When I fly I depend upon my own skill, not subject to the variables of other drivers or blown tires at high speed or railroad crossing signs that are out of order at the wrong moments. After I learn my airplane, it is, with its emergency procedures and the waiting ejection seat, many times more safe than driving a car.

Four minutes to Wiesbaden. Smooth crosscheck. Smooth air. I relax and drift with the smoothness across the river of time.

When I was a boy I lived in a town that would last from now to now as I fly at 500 knots. I rode a bicycle, went to school, worked at odd jobs, spent a few hours at the airport watching the airplanes come and go. Fly one myself? Never. Too hard for me. Too complicated.

But the day came that I had behind me the typical history of a typical aviation cadet. I did not make straight A's in my first college year and I thought that campus life was not the best road to education. For a reason that I still do not know I walked into a recruiting office and told the man behind the desk that I wanted to be an Air Force pilot. I did not know just what it was to be an Air Force pilot, but it had something to do with excitement and adventure, and I would have begun Life.

To my surprise, I passed the tests. I matched the little airplanes in the drawings to the ones in the photographs. I identified which terrain was actually shown in Map Two. I wrote that Gear K will rotate counterclockwise if Lever A is pushed forward. The doctors poked at me, discovered that I was breathing constantly, and all of a sudden I was offered the chance to become a United States Air Force Aviation Cadet. I took the chance.

I raised my right hand and discovered that my name was New Aviation Cadet Bach, Richard D.; A-D One Nine Five Six Three Three One Two. Sir.

For three months I got nothing but a life on the ground. I learned about marching and running and how to fire the 45-caliber pistol. Every once in a while I saw an airplane fly over my training base.

The other cadets came from a strangely similar background. Most of them had never been in an airplane, most of them had tried some form of higher education and did not succeed at it. They decided on Excitement and Adventure. They sweated in the Texas sun with me and they

memorized the General Orders and Washington's Address
and the Aviation Cadet Honor Code. They were young
enough to take the life without writing exposés or telling the
squadron commander that they had had enough of this
heavy-handed treatment from the upper class. In time we
became the upper class and put a stripe or two on our
shoulderboards and learned about being heavy-handed with
the lower class. If they can't take a little chewing out or a
few minutes of silly games, they'll never make good pilots.

LOOK HERE MISTER DO YOU THINK THIS JOKE'S A PRO-
GRAM? ARE YOU SMILING, MISTER? ARE YOU SHOWING EMO-
TION? MAINTAIN EYE-TO-EYE CONTACT WITH ME, MISTER!
DON'T YOU HAVE ANY CONTROL OVER YOURSELF? GOD HELP
THE UNITED STATES OF AMERICA IF YOU EVER BECOME AN
AIR FORCE PILOT!

And then, suddenly, Preflight Training was over and we
were on our way to become the lower class at a base where
we began to learn about airplanes, and where we first
breathed the aluminum-rubber-paint-oil-parachute air of
an airplane cockpit and where we began to get a tiny secret
idea, shared in secret by every other cadet in the class, that
an airplane is actually a living thing, that loves to fly.

I took the academics and I loved the flying and I bore
the military inspections and the parades for six months.
Then I left Primary Flight School to become part of the
lower class in Basic Flight School, where I was introduced
to the world of turbine and speed and spent my first day
in Basic Single-Engine Flight School.

Everything is new fresh exciting imminent tangible. A
sign: *Cadet Club;* rows of tarpapered barracks; close-cut
brown grass; weedless sidewalks; hot sun; bright sun; blue
sky, ceilingless and free above my polished hatbill and
stripeless shoulderboards. A strange face above white-

banded boards and a set of white gloves. "Fall in, gentlemen."

A flight of four sun-burnished silver jet training planes whistle over the base. Jets. "Let's expedite, gentlemen, fall in."

In we fall. "Welcome back to the Air Force, gentlemen, this is Basic." A pause. Distant crackle of full throttle and takeoff. "You tigers will get your stripes here. It's not a lot of fun or a no-sweat program. If you can't hack it, you're out. So you were Cadet Group Commander in Primary; you let up, you slack the books, you're out. Stay sharp and you'll make it. LaiUFF, HAICE! Ho-ward, HAR!"

The B-4 bag is heavy in the right hand. Dust on shined shoes. Hot air doesn't cool as I move through it. Black rubber heels on dusty asphalt. Away, a lone jet trainer heads for the runway. Solo. I am a long way from Primary Flight School. A long way from the chug of a T-28's butterpaddle propeller. And a long way still from the silver wings above the left breast pocket. Where are the hills? Where is the green? The cool air? In Primary Flight School. This is Texas. This is Basic.

". . . program will require hard work . . ." says the wing commander.

". . . and you'd best stay sharp in my squadron . . ." says the squadron commander.

"This is your barracks," says the whitegloves. "There are T-33 pilot's handbooks in every room. Learn the emergency procedures. All of them. You will be asked. Another whitegloves will be around later to answer questions."

Questions.

"Inspections every Saturday?"

"Are the classes tough?"

"What is the airplane like?"

"When do we fly?"

A cold night in a white-collar bed. Cold twinkle of familiar stars through the window. Talk in the dark barracks.

"Just think, boy, jets at last!"

"So it's tough. They'll have to throw me out. I'll never quit because it's hard."

". . . airspeed down final with the gun bay doors open is one twenty plus fuel plus ten, right?"

"Let's see, Johnny, is that 'climb to twenty-five thousand and rock wings'? Twenty-five thousand feet! Man, we're flying JETS!"

"Never thought I'd make it to Basic. We've come a long way from Preflight . . ."

Behind the quiet talk is the roar of night-flying turbines as the upper class learns, and the flash of landing lights bright for an instant on the wall opposite my open window.

Tenuous sleep. Upperclass voices by the window as they return in the night. "I never saw *that* before! He only had ninety-five percent and his tailpipe was bright red . . . really red!"

". . . so then Mobile told me to climb in Sector One to thirty thousand feet. I couldn't even find the field, let alone Sector One . . ."

My glowing Air Force watch says 0300. Strange dreams. The beautiful blonde looks up at me. She asks a question. "What's your airspeed turning base leg with three hundred and fifty gallons of fuel on board?" A crowded and fantastically complex instrument panel, with a huge altimeter pointing to 30,000. Helmets with visors, red-topped ejection seats, instruments, instruments.

Sleep soaks away into the pillow and the night is still and dark. What do I do with a zero loadmeter reading?

Battery *off* . . . no . . . battery on . . . nono . . . "activate electrical device" . . . Outside, the green beam and the split white beam of the beacon on the control tower go round and round and round.

But once again the days pass and I learn. I am concerned with ground schools and lectures; with first flights in the T-33; and after ten hours aloft with an instructor in the back seat, with flying it alone. Then with instruments and precise control of an airplane in any weather. With formation. With navigation.

It would all be a great deal of fun if I knew for certain that I would successfully finish Basic Training and wear at last the silver wings. But when instrument flying is new, it is difficult, and my class that numbered 112 in Preflight is now cut to 63. None have been killed in airplane crashes, none have bailed out or ejected from an airplane. For one reason or another, for academic or military or flying deficiencies, or sometimes just because he has had enough of the tightly-controlled routine, a cadet will pack his B-4 bag one evening and disappear into the giant that is the Air Force.

I had expected some not to finish the program, but I had expected them to fail in a violent sheet of flame or in a bright spinning cloud of fragments of a midair collision.

There are near-misses. I am flying as Lead in a four-ship flight of T-33's. With 375 knots and a clear sky overhead, I press the control stick back to begin a loop. Our airplanes are just passing the vertical, noses high in the blue sky, when a sudden flash of blurred silver streaks across our path, and is gone. I finish the loop, wingmen faithfully watching only my airplane and working hard to stay in their positions, and twist in my seat to see the airplane that nearly took all four of us out of the sky. But it is gone as surely and as completely as if it had never been. There had not been time for reaction or fear or where did he come from. There had simply been a silver flash ahead of me in the sky. I think about it for a moment and begin another loop.

A few weeks later it happened to a lowerclass cadet, practicing acrobatics alone at 20,000 feet. "I was on top of a Cuban Eight, just starting down, when I felt a little thud. When I rolled out, I saw that my right tiptank was gone and that the end of the wing was pretty well shredded. I thought I'd better come back home."

He didn't even see the flash of the airplane that hit him. After he had landed and told what had happened, the base settled down to wait for the other airplane. In a little more than an hour, one airplane of all the airplanes on mobile control's list of takeoffs failed to have an hour written in the column marked "Return." Search airplanes went up arrowing through the dust like swift efficient robots seeking a fallen member of the clan. The darkness fell, and the robots found nothing.

The base was quiet and held its breath. Cadet dining halls were still, during the evening meal. Not everyone is home tonight. Pass the salt please, Johnny. The clink of stamped steel forks on mass-fired pottery. I hear it was an upperclassman in the other squadron. Muted clinks, voices low. Across the room, a smile. He should be calling in any minute now. Anybody want some more milk? You can't kill an upperclassman.

The next day, around the square olive-drab briefing tables in the flight shack, we got the official word. You can kill an upperclassman. Let's look around, gentlemen; remember that there are sixty airplanes from this base alone in the sky during the day. You're not bomber pilots here, keep that head on a swivel and never stop looking around.

And we briefed and flew our next mission.

Then, suddenly, we had made it. A long early morning, a crisp formation of the lower class in review as we stand at parade rest, a sixteen-ship flyby, a speech by a general and by the base commander.

They return my salute, shake my hand, present me a cold set of small wings that flash a tiny beam of silver. I made it all the way through. Alive. Then there are orders to advanced flying training and the glory-soaked number that goes F-84F. I am a pilot. A rated Air Force pilot. A fighter pilot.

The German night is full around me, and in my soft earphones is solid hard static from the blue fire that sluices across the windscreen and across the low-frequency antenna in the belly of my airplane. The slim needle of the radiocompass is becoming more and more excited, jerking to the right, always to the right of course; trembling for a second there, swinging back toward Spangdahlem behind me, jerking again toward my right wingtip. I am glad again for the TACAN.

The air is still and smooth as velvet glass, but I tighten again my safety belt and shoulder harness and turn up the cockpit lights. Bright light, they like to say in the ground schools, destroys night vision. Tonight it does not make any difference, for there is nothing to see outside the plexiglass, and the bright light makes it easier to read the instruments. And in the brightness I will not be blinded by lightning. I am strapped in, my gloves are on, my helmet chin strap is fastened, my flight jacket is zipped, my boots are firm and comfortable. I am ready for whatever the weather has to offer me. For a moment I feel as if I should push the gun switch to *guns,* but it is an irrational fleeting thought. I check again the defroster on, pitot heat on, engine screens retracted. Come and get me, storm. But the air is still and smooth; I have minute after minute of valuable weather time ticking away, adding to the requirement for an advanced instrument rating.

I am foolish. Here I am as nervous as a cat, thinking of a storm that has probably already died away off course. And above 30,000 feet even the worst storms are not so violent as they are at lower altitudes. As I remember, it is rare to find much hail at high altitudes in storms, and lightning has never been shown to be the direct cause of any airplane crash. These elaborate precautions are going to look childish after I land in half an hour at Chaumont and walk up the creaky wooden stairway to my room and take off my boots and finish my letter home. In two hours I will be sound asleep.

Still, it will be good to get this flight over with. I would never make a good all-weather interceptor pilot. Perhaps with training I could become accustomed to hours and hours of weather and storms, but at this moment I am quite happy with my fighter-bomber and the job of shooting at things that I can see.

I have heard that interceptor pilots are not even allowed to roll their airplanes: hard on the electronic gear. What a dismal way to make a living, straight and level and solid instruments all the time. Poor guys.

I might, just a little, envy the F-106 pilot his big delta-wing interceptor. And he might, just a little, envy me my mission. He has the latest airplane and an engine filled with sheer speed. His great grey delta would make a good air combat plane, but he flies day on day of hooded attacks toward dots of smoky green light on his radar screen. My

'84F is older and slower and soon to be changed from sculptured aluminum to a seamless swept memory, but my mission is one of the best missions that a fighter pilot can fly.

FAC, for instance. Pronounced fack. Forward Air Controller. The blast of low-level and gunsight on the truck columns of the Aggressor. FAC. "Checkmate, Bipod Delta here. I've got a bunch of troops and two tanks coming toward my position. They're on the high ground just south of the castle on the dirt road. You got 'em in sight?"

The greening hills of Germany below me, the chessboard in another war game. What a job for a fighter pilot, to be a FAC. Stuck out with the Army in the mud with a jeep and a radio transmitter, watching your friends come in on the strikes. "Roj, Delta. Got the castle and the road in sight, not the target." A sprinkling of dots in the grass by the road. "As you were, got 'em in sight. Take your spacing, Two."

"What's your armament, Checkmate?"

"Simulated napalm and guns. First pass will be the napalm."

"Hurry up, will you? The tanks are pouring on the coal; must have seen you."

"Roj."

I melt into stick and throttle, my airplane leaps ahead and hurls itself in a sweeping burst of speed at the road. There are the tanks, feathers of dust and grass spraying long behind their tracks. But it is as if they were caught in cooling wax, I move fifteen times faster than they. Take it down to the deck, attacking from behind the tank. In its wax, it begins to turn, grass spewing from beneath its right track. I bank my wings, ever so slightly, and feel confident, omnipotent, as an eagle plunging from height to mouse. Men are riding on the tank, clutching handholds. They do not hear me, but they see me, looking back over their camouflaged shoulders. And I see them. What a way to make a living, clinging with all your strength to the back of a 50-ton block of steel hurtling across a meadow. In the time it takes me to count three, the tank, frozen in its turn, frames itself for a moment in my windscreen, and the lowest diamond of my gunsight flicks through it and my thumb has released the imaginary tanks of jellied gasoline from beneath the wings. Wouldn't be a tank driver in wartime for all the money in the world. Pull up. Hard turn right. Look back. The tank is rolling to a stop, obedient to the rules of our game. Two is snapping his black swept shadow over the hatch of the second tank. Tanks make such easy targets. I guess they just hope that they won't get caught in an air strike. "Nice job, Checkmate. Work over the troops, will you?" A friendly request, from a man who is seeing from the ground the sight that so often has been caught in his forward windscreen. In the war we would worry now about small-arms fire and shoulder-mounted antiaircraft missiles, but we would already have decided that when our time comes, it will come, and the worry would be a transient one. Down on the troops. Most unwarlike troops, these. Knowing the game, and not often having the chance for their own private and special airshow, they stand and watch us come in. One raises his arms in a defiant V. I bank again, very slightly, to hurtle directly toward him. He and I have a little personal clash of wills. Low. I climb up the slope of the long meadow toward my antagonist. If there are telephone wires across the meadow, I will have plenty of clearance going beneath them. In war, my antagonist would be caught in the hail of Armor Piercing Incendiary from six Browning 50-caliber machine guns. But though this is not real war, it is a real challenge he throws to me. I dare you to make me duck. We are all such little boys at heart. I make one last tiny adjustment so that my drop tanks will pass on either side of his outflung hands if he does not duck. I see the arms begin to falter as he flicks from sight beneath the nose. If he hasn't ducked, he is due for a flattening burst of jetblast. But he does have determination, this man. Usually we scatter the troops like flocks of chicks around the hilltops. I turn on another pass from another direction, looking, from sudden height of my pullup, for my friend. One dot looks like another.

Another pass, carried perhaps a little too low, for my friend dives for the ground even before I pass over him. That is really very profound. One dot looks like another. You can't tell good from evil when you move 500 feet per second above the grass. You can only tell that the dots are men.

On one FAC mission near the hem of the iron curtain we were asked to fly east for two minutes in order to find our Controller. Two minutes east would have put us over the border and into Soviet airspace. Enemy airspace. The Controller had meant to say "west." The hills did not look any different on the Other Side. As we circled and turned west I had looked across into the forbidden land. I saw no fences, no iron curtains, no strange coloring of the earth. Only the green rolling of the constant hills, a scattering of little grey villages. Without my compass and map, with the East-West border heavily penciled in red, I would have thought that the villages of men that I saw in the east were just as the villages of the west. Fortunately, I had the map.

"How about a high-speed run for the troops, Checkmate?"

"Sure thing," I say, smiling. For the troops. If I were a fighter pilot marooned on the ground with the olive-drab Army, nothing would ease my solitude quite so much as the 500-knot rapport with my friends and their airplanes. So, a pass for the troops. "Open her up, Checkmate." And throttle full open, engine drinking fuel at 7,000 pounds per hour. Across the meadow, faster than an arrow from a hundred-pound bow, heading this time for the cluster of dots by the radio-jeep of the FAC. 510 knots and I am joy. They love my airplane. See her beauty. See her speed. And I, too, love my airplane. A whiplash and the FAC and his jeep are gone. Pull up, far up, nose high in the milkblue sky. And we roll. Earth and sky joyously twined in a blur of dwindling emerald and turquoise. Stop the roll swiftly, upside down, bring the nose again through the horizon, roll back to straight and level. The sky is a place for living and for whistling and for singing and for dying. It is a place that is built to give people a place from which to look down on all the others. It is always fresh and awake and clear and cold, for when the cloud covers the sky or fills the place where the sky should be, the sky is gone. The sky is a place where the air is ice and you breathe it and you live it and you wish that you could float and dream and race and play all the days of your life. The sky is there for everyone, yet only a few seek it out. It is all color, all heat and cold, all oxygen and forest leaves and sweet air and salt air and fresh crystal air that has never been breathed before. The sky whirs around you, keening and hissing over your head and face and it gets in your eyes and numbs your ears in a coldness that is bright and sharp. You can drink it and chew it and swallow it. You can rip your fingers through the rush of sky and the hard wind. It is your very life inside you and over your head and beneath your feet. You shout a song and the sky sweeps it away, twisting it and tumbling it through the hard liquid air. You can climb to the top of it, fall with it twisting and rushing around you, leap clear, arms wide, catching the air with your teeth. It holds the stars at night as strongly as it holds the brazen sun in the day. You shout a laugh of joy, and the rush of wind is there to carry the laugh a thousand miles.

In my climbing roll away from the FAC, I love everyone. Which, however, will not prevent me from killing them. If that day comes.

"Very nice show, Checkmate."

"Why, feel free to call on us at any time, Bravo." So this is joy. Joy fills the whole body, doesn't it? Even my toes are joyful. For this the Air Force finds it necessary to pay me. No. They do not pay me for the hours that I fly. They pay me for the hours that I do not fly; those hours chained to the ground are the ones in which pilots earn their pay.

I and the few thousand other single-engine pilots live in a system that has been called a close fraternity. I have heard more than once the phrase "arrogant fighter pilots." Oddly enough as generalizations go, they are both well chosen phrases.

A multiengine bomber pilot or a transport pilot or a navigator or a nonflying Air Force officer is still, basically, a human being. But it is a realization that I must strive to achieve, and in practice, unless it is necessary, I do not talk to them. There have been a few multiengine pilots stationed at bases where I have been in the past. They are happy to fly big lumbering airplanes and live in a world of low altitudes and long flights and coffee and sandwiches on the flight deck. It is just this contentment with the droning adventureless existence that sets them apart from single-engine pilots.

I belong to a group of men who fly alone. There is only one seat in the cockpit of a fighter airplane; there is no space allotted for another pilot to tune the radios in the weather or make the calls to air traffic control centers or to

[123]

help with the emergency procedures or to call off the airspeed down final approach. There is no one else to break the solitude of a long crosscountry flight. There is no one else to make decisions. I do everything myself, from engine start to engine shutdown. In a war, I will face alone the missiles and the flak and the small-arms fire over the front lines. If I die, I will die alone.

Because of this, and because this is the only way that I would have it, I do not choose to spend my time with the multiengine pilots who live behind the lines of adventure. It is an arrogant attitude and unfair. The difference between one pilot in the cockpit and many on the flight deck should not be enough to cause them never to associate. But there is an impassable barrier between me and the man who prefers the life of low and slow.

I ventured, once, to break the barrier. I talked one evening to a pilot in a Guard squadron that had been forced to trade its F-86H's for four-engine transports. If there ever was a common bond between single- and multiengine flying, I could see it through the eyes of this man. "How do you like multi after the *Sabre?*" I had asked, lights dancing on the pool beside the officers' club.

I had picked the wrong pilot. He was new in the squadron, a transfer.

"I've never flown an eighty-six and I have no desire to fly one," he said.

The word "eighty-six" sounded strange and foreign in his mouth, words not often said. I discovered that there had been a complete turnover of pilots in that squadron when its airplane changed from fighter-interceptor to heavy transport, and that my partner in conversation had a multiengine mind. The silver wings above his pocket were cast in the same mold that mine had been, but he lived in another world, behind a wall that has no gate. It has been months since that evening, and I have not since bothered to speak with a multiengine pilot.

Every so often a single-engine pilot is caught in a web of circumstance that transfers him from a fighter squadron into the ranks of multiengine pilots, that forces him to learn about torque pressure and overhead switch panels and propeller feathering procedures. I have known three of these. They fought furiously against the change, to no avail. For a short while they flew multiengine airplanes with their single-engine minds, but in less than a year all three had been released from active Air Force duty at their own request.

The program that switched fighter pilots into transports had once been quite active, affecting hundreds of single-engine pilots. Shortly after, perhaps by coincidence, I had read an article that deplored the loss of young Air Force pilots to civilian life. I would gladly have bet that some interesting statistics awaited the man who first probed the retention rate of fighter pilots forced to fly multiengine aircraft. The code of the Air Force is that any officer should be able to adapt to any position assigned him, but the code does not recognize the tremendous chasm between the background and attitude of single- and multiengine pilots.

The solitude that each fighter pilot knows when he is alone with his airplane is the quality that shows him that his airplane is actually a thing of life. Life exists in multiengine airplanes, too, but it is more difficult to find through the talk of crew on interphone and how are the passengers taking the rough air and crew chief can you pass me up a flight lunch. It is sacrilege to eat while you fly an airplane.

Solitude is that key that says that life is not confined to things that grow from the earth. The interdependence of pilot and airplane in flight shows that each cannot exist without the other, that we truly depend upon each other for our very existence. And we are confident in each other. One fighter squadron motto sums up the attitude of fighter pilots everywhere; *We can beat any man in any land in any game that he can name for any amount that he can count.*

In contrast, I read on the wall of Base Operations at a multiengine base: *The difficult we approach with caution. The impossible we do not attempt.* I could not believe it. I thought that it must have been someone's idea of a joke for the day. But the sign was neatly lettered and a little grey, as if it had been there for a long while. It was joy to spin the dust of that runway from my wheels and to be out again in a sky designed for fighter pilots.

It is from pride that my arrogance comes. I have a history of sacrifice and of triumph and of pride. As the pilot of my *Thunderstreak,* in charge of an airplane built to rocket and bomb and strafe the enemy on the ground, my history goes back to the men who flew the P-47's, the *Thunderbolts* of the Second World War. The same hills that are buried beneath me tonight remember the stocky, square-cut Jug of twenty years ago, and the concrete silos that were flak towers still bear the bulletholes of its low-level attack and its eight 50-caliber machine guns.

After the Jug pilots of Europe came the Hog pilots of Korea to face the rising curtain of steel from the ground. They flew another Republic airplane: the straight-wing F-84G *Thunderjet,* and they played daily games of chance with the flak and the rifle bullets and the cables across the valleys and the MiGs that crept past the '86's on the patrol. There are not a great many '84G pilots of Korea who lived through their games, as, if a war breaks out in Europe tomorrow, there will not be a great many '84F pilots surviving.

After me and my Superhog are the F-100D *Super Sabre* pilots that have waited out the years of cold war on alert all around the world. And after them, the men who fly the Ultimate Hog, the F-105D *Thunderchief*, who can attack targets on the ground, through weather, by radar alone.

My airplane and I are part of a long chain from the mist of the past to the mist of the future. We are even now obsolete; but if a war should begin on the imminent tomorrow, we will be, at least, bravely obsolete.

We fill the squares of our training board with black X's in grease pencil on the acetate overlay; X's in columns headed "Low-level navigation without radio aids" and "Combat profile" and "Max-load takeoff." Yet we are certain that we will not all survive the next war.

Coldly, factually, it is stated that we are not only flying against the small-arms and the cables and the flak, but against the new mechanics in the nose of a ground-to-air missile as well. I have often thought, after watching the movies of our ground-to-air missiles in action, that I am glad I am not a Russian fighter-bomber pilot. I wonder if there is also a Russian pilot, after seeing his own movies, with thanks in his heart that he is not an American fighter-bomber pilot.

We talk about the missiles every once in a while, discussing the fact of their existence and the various methods of dodging them. But dodging is predicated on knowing that they are chasing, and during a strike we will be concentrating on the target, not on worrying about the fire or the flak or the missiles thrown up against us. We will combine our defense with our offense, and we will hope.

Speaking factually, we remind ourselves that our airplanes can still put almost as much ordnance on the target as any other fighter available. It does it without the finesse of the F-105's radar, we say, but the fire eventually reaches

[127]

the target. Our words are for the most part true, but there is a long mental battle to submerge the also-true words that our airplane is old, and was designed to fight in another era of warfare. We fly with a bravely buried sense of inferiority. As Americans, we should fly modern American airplanes. There is no older or slower ground support airplane in any NATO Air Force than ours.

The French fly F-84F's, but they are transitioning now into *Mirages* and *Vautours* built for modern sky. The Luftwaffe is flying F-84F's, but they are well into the task of converting to Maltese-crossed F-104G's. The Canadians are flying Mark VI *Sabres,* contemporary with the '84F, and they are changing now to their own CF-104G.

We fly our '84F's and the never-ending rumors of airplanes to come. We will get F-100D's soon. We will get F-104's soon. We will get the Navy's F4H's soon. We will be in F-105's before the year is up.

There is, somewhere, a later airplane scheduled and waiting for us. But it has not yet shown its face and we do not talk about our shortcomings. We make do with what we have, as the P-39 pilots and the P-40 pilots did at the beginning of the Second War.

The pilots in my squadron today are as varied a group of men as could be netted at a random stroke into the waters of civilian life. There is a young second lieutenant, a housewares salesman, just accumulating the first fine scratches on his golden bars. There is a major who flew Mustangs and Jugs on long-ago fighter sweeps into Germany. There is a lawyer, practice established; a computer engineer; three airline pilots; two bachelors whose only income came from Guard flying. There are the successful and the unsuccessful. The unruffled and the volatile. The readers of books and the seekers of adventure.

If you looked closely you would find constants that many share: most are within five years of 30, most are family men, most have served their years of active duty with the regular Air Force. But one constant, without exception, they are all men of action. The most introspective pilot in the squadron leaves his book, carefully marked, in his BOQ room, and straps himself each day to 25,000 pounds of fighter airplane. He leads a flight of four airplanes through patterns of bombing and strafing and rocket firing and nuclear weapon delivery. He makes wing takeoffs into 500-foot weather ceilings and doesn't see the ground again until he breaks out of the ragged cloud and freezing rain two hours and 900 miles from his takeoff runway. He alternates his letters to his family with an occasional review of airborne emergency procedures, and, occasionally, puts them to use when a red warning light flares in his cockpit, or his nosewheel fails to extend when it is time to land. There are those who speak loudly, and perhaps with too little humility, but those same back their words with action every time they step into an airplane. There are nights in the officers' club when whiskey glasses splinter against the rough stone walls, there are colored smoke bombs thrown into the closed rooms of sleeping comrades, there is a song, not altogether complimentary, sung of the wing commander.

But you can count on the coming of the dawn, and with it the concussion of engine start in the cold wind. Take First Lieutenant Roger Smith, for instance, who last night deftly introduced four lighted firecrackers into the wing materiel officer's room. Grounds, really, for court-martial. But in the confusion he was not identified, and this morning he flies number Two in a ground support mission against the Aggressor Force at Hohenfels. You cannot tell him, under oxygen mask and lowered visor, from Captain Jim Davidson, flight leader, calling now for radar vector to the target area. Davidson spent the night writing to his wife, and telling her, among other things, that he did not have any real reason to believe that the squadron would be released from active duty before the assigned year of duty was finished. In close formation the two swept fighters drop from altitude, indicating the same 450 knots on identical airspeed indicators. "Tank column at ten o'clock low," Davidson calls. And they turn together to the attack.

Men of action, and every day, new action. In the gloved right hand, the possibility of life and death.

The loud slurred drawl harassing the multiengine pilot at the bar belongs to a man named Roudabush, who, a year ago, against all regulations, landed a flamed-out fighter at night, without electrical power and therefore without lights, at an airport in Virginia. He refused to bail out of his airplane or even to jettison his external fuel tanks over the city of Norfolk, and was reprimanded.

"You tell yourself that you'll bail out if the thing quits at night," he said once, "but when you look down and see all the lights of the city . . . kinda changes your mind." A man like that, you don't care how he talks. You fly with him, and it makes you proud.

Johnny Blair, leaning against the mahogany bartop swirling the icecubes in his glass and smiling faintly at Roudabush's banter, has a little scar on his jaw. Shortly past noon on one day in his life he was beginning a LABS run, 500 knots toward the target, 100 feet in the air, when he heard a thud and the overheat and fire warning lights came on. He pulled up, heard another thud, and the cockpit filled with smoke. Without a word to his wingman, he shut down his engine, jettisoned the canopy, and squeezed the trigger on the right handgrip. For a few seconds in the afternoon he fought to release himself from the tumbling steel seat, 800 feet over a forest of pine. The automatic parachute release failed. That inward person immediately pulled the manual parachute release, with the world spinning green and blue about him. He swung one time in the harness before he dragged through the treetops and was slammed to the ground. He lost his helmet and mask in the bailout, and an anonymous tree-branch slashed his jaw. Then it was over, the inner man subsiding, the outward man spreading the parachute canopy as a signal to the helicopters, suffering slightly from shock, and telling the story very plainly and undramatically to whomever could benefit from it. Otherwise he does not talk of it, and except for the scar, he is the sort of person who would lead you to say, "Now there is a typical high-school geometry teacher." Which, of course, is exactly what he is.

It takes a while to learn to know many of these men as friends, for many of them, in the fear of being thought braggart or self-styled supermen, do not tell of narrow escapes and brushes with disaster to anyone who inquires. Gradually, with much time, the newcomer to the squadron discovers that Blair had an interesting low-altitude bailout, that Roudabush "coulda kissed that bitch" when his airplane stretched its glide, in the dark, to the Virginia runway; that Travas ran into an air-to-air target in the days when they were made of plastic rag and steel bars, and dragged 70 pounds of steel and 30 feet of polyethylene home, imbedded in his wing.

And the squadron learns, gradually, that the newcomer has had his own share of experience in the world above the ground. A squadron is a swirling multicolored pool of experience, from which is painted the freewheeling sweep of life in the air, in individual brushstrokes. The brilliant shimmering brass of combat in the sun burns itself into the pilots in their cockpit; dark sky and dark sea soak their enormous blue into the man who guides his airplane between them; and, once in a very long while, the scarlet of a fireball against a mountainside glares to outshine all the other hues, in time breaking to tiny sharp sparkles of pain that never quite disappear.

I reach to my right in the red darkness and turn the volume of the radiocompass as low as it will go. It reports now only fragments of the Spangdahlem callsign behind me, and has become more of a thunderstorm indicator than a navigation radio. This is not bad, with the TACAN working well, and I am glad to have a thunderstorm indicator that is so reliable. There is a dim flash in the grey to my right, a momentary suggestion of light that is instantly gone again.

Tuning down the radiocompass was a short break, and the routine of the crosscheck continues. Straight and level. Attitude and airspeed. Needle and ball. No swerving from the target. As if I had a Shape under my wing.

There are Shapes and there are Bugs and there are Blue Boys, all names for the form that houses a few million tightly-controlled neutrons that make an atomic bomb. Or more properly, a Nuclear Device. It is always called a Device.

The first mission of many squadrons of tactical fighters is now a strategic one, and the numbers of many fighter wings are followed by the ominous letters *SD*.

SD stands for Special Delivery, and means that pilots spend hours studying targets of remote corners of the world and learning selected bits of nuclear physics and building their language to include LABS and Shape and Nuke and the meaning of the T-Zero light. They fly a strange new

[132]

bombing pattern in their practice, they fly it alone, and only the first bomb counts for score. A pilot away from a fighter cockpit since Korea would not recognize a full panel of switches and lights for the nuclear weapons delivery system. But it is an important panel, today.

Part of my job is to know how to deliver a Shape, and I practice it dutifully. The placing of Device on Target begins with a swirl of charts and dividers and angles and measurements. From that emerge a few highly-classified figures that are given for the nourishment of a pair of computers mounted in my airplane.

Normally, the missions are flown with only a small 25-pound practice bomb to record the effectiveness of the delivery, but once a year I am required to fly with a full-size, full-weight Shape under my left wing. This is to remind me that when I carry a real atomic bomb, I will have to hold a bit of right stick-pressure to keep the wings level on take-off.

A practice Shape is smooth and streamlined and not unpretty. The real Device, which looks exactly the same, is the ugliest mass of metal that I have ever seen. Blunt-nosed, olive-drab and heavy, it is like a greedy deformed remora attached to the smooth swept wing of my airplane.

With every other pilot in the squadron, I joined the Air National Guard because I like to fly airplanes. With strafing and rocketing and conventional bombing, of course, our mission passes the realm of mere airplane-flying and becomes one of destroying enemy machines and enemy troops. But the mounting of a Device on the airplane is, as far as the pilots are concerned, one step too many. I do not like it at all, yet the Shape is a part of my mission, and I learn to toss it and hit a target.

Hold the right stick-pressure, and gear up and flaps up

and low-level to the target. The trees flick by below, the sky is the same French sky that I have flown for months, the cockpit is the same about me, and I cannot see the Device under my wing. But the lights on its control box glimmer fully in front of me, and I am acutely aware of its nearness. I feel as if I am standing near a lightly-chained gorilla as it awakens. I do not care for gorillas.

The lights tell me that the Device is awakening, and I respond by pushing up the proper switches at the proper moments. The Initial Point rushes in at me from the horizon, and I push my distaste for the monster to the back of my mind as I set another panel of switches in the last combination of steps that lead to its release. One hundred percent rpm.

The last red-roofed village flashes below me, and the target, a pyramid of white barrels, is just visible at the end of its run-in line. Five hundred knots. Switch down, button pressed. Timers begin their timing, circuits are alerted for the drop. Inch down to treetop altitude. I do not often fly at 500 knots on the deck, and it is apparent that I am moving quickly. The barrels inflate. I see that their white paint is flaking. And the pyramid streaks beneath me. Back on the stick smoothly firmly to read four G on the accelerometer and center the needles of the indicator that is only used in nuke weapon drops and center them and hold it there and I'll bet those computers are grinding their little hearts out and all I can see is sky in the windscreen hold the G's keep the needles centered there's the sun going beneath me and WHAM.

My airplane rolls hard to the right and tucks more tightly into her loop and strains ahead even though we are upside down. The Shape has released me more than I have released it. The little white barrels are now six thousand feet directly beneath my canopy. I have no way to tell if it was a good drop or not. That was decided back with the charts and graphs and the dividers and the angles. I kept the needles centered, the computers did their task automatically, and the Device is on its way.

Now, while it is still in the air and climbing with the inertia that my airplane has given it, my job becomes one of escape. Hold the throttle at the firewall, pull the nose down until it is well below the horizon, roll back so that the sun is over my head, and run. If the Shape were packed with neutrons instead of concrete ballast, I would need every moment I could find for my escape, for every moment is another foot away from the sun-blast that would just as easily destroy a friendly F-84F as it would the hostile target. Visor down against the glare-that-would-be, turn the rear-view mirror away, crouch down in the seat and fly as fast as possible toward Our Side.

At the same moment, the Device has stopped in the air, at the very apex of its high trajectory. A long plumbline descended would pass through the center of the white pyramid. Then it falls. Subject only to the winds, impossible to halt, the bomb falls. If it were a real Device in a real war, it would be well at this time for the enemy to have his affairs in order. The hate of the enemy has been reflected in the hate of the friend, reflected through me and my airplane and the computers that it carries.

And it is too late. We may declare an armistice, we may suddenly realize that the people under the bomb suspended are truly, deeply, our friends and our brothers. We may suddenly, blindingly see the foolishness of our differences, and the means to their solution. But the Device has begun to fall.

Do I feel sorry? Do I feel a certain sadness? I have felt

those from the moment I saw the first practice Shape lifted into position under my wing.

But I love my airplane more than I hate the Device. I am the lens through which the hatred of my country is focused into a bright molten ball over the home of the enemy.

Although it is my duty and my only desire in wartime to serve my country as best I can, I rationalize. We will never really use the Devices. My targets will be completely and solely military ones. Everyone who is consumed in the fire is purely evil and filled with hatred for freedom.

There is a point where even the most ardent rationalization is only a gesture. I hope, simply, that I will never have to throw one of the repellent things at living people.

The distance-measuring drum of the steady TACAN has turned down now to 006 and that is as far as it will go, for I am six miles into the deep night directly above the transmitter of the Wiesbaden TACAN station. I am a minute and a half behind schedule in a wind that came from nowhere. In 30 minutes my wheels will be touching the cold wet runway at Chaumont Air Base.

The thought would have been reassuring, but there are two quick flashes of lightning to the right, across my course.

Once again, ready the report, tilt the stick to the right, fly the instruments, fly the instruments, thumb down on microphone button.

CHAPTER FIVE

"Rhein Control, Air Force Jet Two Niner Four Zero Five, Wiesbaden." The City That Was Not Bombed.

Silence. Here we go again. "Rhein Control, Rhein control; Air Force Jet . . . " I try once. Twice. Three times. There is no answer. I am alone with my instruments, and suddenly aware of my aloneness.

Click around with the radio channel selector under my right glove; perhaps I can talk to Barber Radar. "Barber Radar, Air Force Jet Two Niner Four Zero Five, over." Once. Twice. Three times. Nothing.

A flash in the clouds ahead. The air is still smooth, paving the way. Hold the heading. Hold the altitude.

A decision in my mind. If I were flying this crosscountry just to get myself home tonight, I would turn back now. I still have enough fuel to return to the clear air over Wethersfield. With my transmitter out, I cannot ask for a radar vector through the storms ahead. If it was not for the sack above the machine guns, I would turn back. But it is there, and at Chaumont there is a wing commander who is trusting me to complete my mission. I will continue.

I can use the radiocompass needle to point out the storms, if worst comes to worst I can dodge them by flying between the flashes. But still it is much more comfortable to be a spot of light on someone's radar screen, listening for sure direction about the white blurs that are the most severe cells of a thunderstorm. One more try, although I am certain now that my UHF radio is completely dead. Click click click to 317.5 megacycles. "Moselle Control, Moselle Control, Jet Zero Five." I have no hope. The feeling is justified, for there is no answer from the many-screened room that is Moselle Radar.

Turn back. Forget the wing commander. You will be killed in the storms.

Fear again, and it is exaggerating, as usual. I will not be killed in any storm. Someone else, perhaps, but not me. I have too much flying experience and I fly too strong an airplane to be killed by the weather.

Flash to the right, small flash to the left. A tiny tongue of turbulence licks at my airplane, making the wings rock slightly. No problem. Forty minutes from now I shall be walking across the ramp through the rain to Squadron Operations, Chaumont Air Base. The TACAN is working well, Phalsbourg is 80 miles ahead.

Friends have been killed. Five years ago, Jason Williams, roommate, when he flew into his strafing target.

I was briefing for an afternoon gunnery training mission, sitting on a chair turned backwards with my G-suit legs unzipped and dangling their own way to the wooden floor of the flight shack. I was there, and around the table were three other pilots who would soon be changing into airplanes. Across the room was another flight briefing for an air combat mission.

I was taking a sip of hot chocolate from a paper cup when the training squadron commander walked into the room, G-suit tossed carelessly over one shoulder.

"Anybody briefing for air-to-ground gunnery?"

I nodded over my cup and pointed to my table.

"I'm going to tell you to take it easy and don't get target fixation and don't fly into the ground." He held a narrow strip of paper in his hand. "Student flew into a target on Range Two this morning. Watch your minimum altitude. Take it easy today, OK?"

I nodded again. "Who was it?"

The squadron commander looked at the paper. "Second Lieutenant Jason Williams."

Like a ton of bricks. Second Lieutenant Jason Williams. Willy. My roommate. Willy of the broad smile and the open mind and the many women. Willy who graduated number four in a class of 60 cadets. Willy the only Negro fighter pilot I had ever known. It is funny. And I smiled and set down my cup.

I was amazed at myself. What is so funny about one of my best friends flying into a target on the desert? I should be sad. Dying is a horrible and terrible thing. I must be sad. I must wince, grit my teeth, say, "Oh, no!"

But I cannot keep from smiling. What is so funny? That

is one way to hit the target? The '84 always was reluctant to change direction in a dive? The odds against the only Negro fighter pilot in all the USAF gunnery school at this moment flying into the ground? Willy's dead. Look sad. Look shocked. Look astounded. But I cannot keep from smiling because it is all so very funny.

The briefing is done and I walk outside and strap my airplane around me and push the throttle forward and go out to strafe the rocks and lizards on Range Number Three. Range Number Two is closed.

It happened again, a few months later. "Did you hear about Billy Yardley?" I had not heard from Bill since we graduated from cadets. "He flew into the side of a mountain on a weather approach to Aviano." A ringing in my ears. Billy Yardley is dead. And I smile. Again the wicked unreasoning uncontrollable smile. A smile of pride? 'I am a better pilot than Jason Williams and Billy Yardley because I am still alive'? Kenneth Sullivan crashed in a helicopter in Greenland. Sully. A fine man, a quiet man, and he died in a spinning cloud of snow and rotor blades. And I smile.

Somehow I am not mad or insane or warped, for I see it once in a while on the faces of others when they hear the ringing in their ears at the death of a friend. They smile, just a little. They think of a friend that knows now what we have wondered since we were old enough to wonder: what is behind the curtain? What comes after this world? Willy knows it, Bill Yardley knows it, Sully knows it. And I do not. My friends are keeping a secret from me. It is a secret that they know and that they will not tell. It is a game. I will know tonight or tomorrow or next month or next year, but I must not know now. A strange game. A funny game. And I smile.

I can find out in a minute. Any day on the range I can

wait two seconds too long in the pullout from the strafing panel. I can deliberately fly at 400 knots into one of the very hard mountains of the French Alps. I can roll the airplane on her back and pull her nose straight down into the ground. The game can be over any time that I want it to be. But there is another game to play that is more interesting, and that is the game of flying airplanes and staying alive. I will one day lose that game and learn the secret of the other; why should I not be patient and play one game at a time? And that is what I do.

We fly our missions every day for weeks that become uneventful months. One day one of us does not come back. Three days ago, a Sunday, I left the pages of manuscript that is this book piled neatly on my desk and left for Squadron Operations to meet a flight briefing time of 1115. The mission before mine on the scheduling board was "Lowlevel," with aircraft numbers and pilots' names.

391—Slack
541—Ulshafer

Ulshafer came back. Slack didn't.

Before he was driven to Wing Headquarters, Ulshafer told us what he knew. The weather had gone from very good to very bad, quickly. There were hills ahead that stretched into the clouds. The two '84F's decided to break off the mission and return to the clear weather, away from the hills. Slack was in the lead. The weather closed in as they began to turn, and Ulshafer lost sight of his leader in the clouds.

"I've lost you, Don. Meet you on top of the weather."
"Roj."

Ulshafer climbed and Slack began to climb.

The wingman was alone above the clouds, and there was no answer to his radio calls. He came back alone. And he

was driven, with the base commander, to Wing Headquarters.

The schedule board changed to:

51-9391—Slack AO 3041248

541—Ulshafer

A map was drawn, with a red square around the place
where they had met the weather, southwest of Clemont-
Ferrand. The ground elevation there changes from 1,000
feet to a jutting mountain peak at 6,188 feet. They had
begun their climb just before the mountain.

We waited in Operations and we looked at our watches.
Don Slack has another 10 minutes of fuel, we told ourselves. But we thought of the peak, that before we did not
even know existed, and of its 6,188 feet of rock. Don Slack
is dead. We call for the search-rescue helicopters, we fret
that the ceiling is too low for us to fly out and look for his
airplane on the mountainside, we think of all the ways that
he could still be alive: down at another airport, with radio
failure, bailed out into a village that has no telephone,
alone with his parachute in some remote forest. "His fuel is
out right now." It doesn't make any difference. We know
that Don Slack is dead.

No official word; helicopters still on their way; but the
operations sergeant is copying the pertinent information
concerning the late Lieutenant Slack's flying time, and the
parachute rack next to mine, with its stenciled name, *Slack*,
is empty of helmet and parachute and mae west. There is
on it only an empty nylon helmet bag, and I look at it for
a long time.

I try to remember what I last said to him. I cannot remember. It was something trivial. I think of the times that
we would jostle each other as we lifted our bulky flying
equipment from the racks at the same time. It got so that

[142]

one of us would have to flatten himself against a wall locker while the other would lift his gear from the rack.

Don had a family at home, he had just bought a new Renault, waiting now outside the door. But these do not impress me as much as the thought that his helmet and chute and mae west are missing from his rack, and that he is scheduled to fly again this afternoon. What arrogant confidence we have when we apply grease pencil to the scheduling board.

The friend whose parachute has hung so long next to mine has become the first recalled Air National Guard pilot to die in Europe.

A shame, a waste, a pity? The fault of the President? If we had not been recalled to active duty and to Europe, Don Slack would not be twisted against a French mountain peak that stands 6,188 feet high. Mrs. Slack could blame the President.

But if Don was not here with his airplane, and all the rest of the Guard with him, there might well have been many more dead Americans in Europe today. Don died in the defense of his country as surely as did the first of the Minutemen, in 1776. And we all, knowingly, play the game.

Tonight I am making a move in that game, moving my token five squares from Wethersfield to Chaumont. I still do not expect to fly into a thunderstorm, for they are isolated ahead, but there is always one section of my mind that is devoted to caution, that considers the events that could cost me the game. That part of my mind has a throttle in it as controllable as the hard black throttle under my left glove. I can pull the caution almost completely back to *off* during air combat and ground support missions. There, it is the mission over all. The horizon can twist and writhe and disappear, the hills of France can flick beneath my molded plexiglass canopy, can move around my airplane as though they were fixed on a spinning sphere about me. There is but one thing fixed in war and practice for war: the target. Caution plays little part. Caution is thrown to the 400-knot wind over my wings and the game is to stop the other airplane, and to burn the convoy.

When the throttle that controls caution is at its normal position, it is a computer weighing risk against result. I do not normally fly under bridges; the risk is not worth the result. Yet low-level navigation missions, at altitudes of 50 feet, do not offend my sense of caution, for the risk of scratching an airplane is worth the result of training, of learning and gaining experience from navigating at altitudes where I cannot see more than two miles ahead.

Every flight is weighed in the balance. If the risk involved outweighs the result to be gained, I am nervous and on edge. This is not an absolute thing that says one flight is Dangerous and another is Safe, it is completely a mental condition. When I am convinced that the balance is in favor of the result I am not afraid, no matter the mission. Carried to extremes, a perfectly normal flight involving takeoff, circling the air base, and landing is dangerous, if I am not authorized to fly one of the government's airplanes that day.

The airplane that I fly has no key or secret combination for starting; I merely ask the crew chief to plug in an auxiliary power unit and I climb into the cockpit and I start the engine. When the power unit is disconnected and I taxi to the runway, there is no one in the world who can stop me if I am determined to fly, and once I am aloft I am the total master of the path of my airplane. If I desire, I can fly at a

20-foot altitude up the Champs Elysées; there is no way that anyone can stop me. The rules, the regulations, the warnings of dire punishment if I am caught buzzing towns means nothing if I am determined to buzz towns. The only control that others can force upon me is after I have landed, after I am separated from my airplane.

But I have learned that it more interesting to play the game when I follow the rules; to make an unauthorized flight would be to defy the rules and run a risk entirely out of proportion to the result of one more flight. Such a flight, though possible, is dangerous.

At the other extreme is the world of wartime combat. There is a bridge over the river. The enemy depends upon the bridge to carry supplies to his army that is killing my army. The enemy has fortified his bridge with antiaircraft guns and antiaircraft missiles and steel cables and barrage balloons and fighter cover. But the bridge, because of its importance, must be destroyed. The result of destroying the bridge is worth the risk of destroying it. The mission is chalked on a green blackboard and the flight is briefed and the bombs and rockets are hung on our airplanes and I start the engine and I take off and I fully intend to destroy the bridge.

In my mind the mission is not a dangerous one; it is one that simply must be done. If I lose the game of staying alive over this bridge, that is just too bad; the bridge is more important than the game.

How slowly it is, though, that we learn of the nature of dying. We form our preconceptions, we make our little fancies of what it is to pass beyond the material, we imagine what it feels like to face death. Every once in a while we actually do face it.

It is a dark night, and I am flying right wing on my flight leader. I wish for a moon, but there is none. Beneath us by some six miles lie cities beginning to sink under a gauzy coverlet of mist. Ahead the mist turns to low fog, and the bright stars dim a fraction in a sheet of high haze. I fly intently on the wing of my leader, who is a pattern of three white lights and one of green. The lights are too bright in the dark night, and surround themselves with brilliant flares of halo that make them painful to watch. I press the microphone button on the throttle. "Go dim on your nav lights, will you, Red Leader?"

"Sure thing."

In a moment the lights are dim, mere smudges of glowing filament that seek more to blend his airplane with the stars than to set it apart from them. His airplane is one of the several whose *dim* is just too dim to fly by. I would rather close my eyes against the glare than fly on a shifting dim constellation moving among the brighter constellations of stars. "Set 'em back to bright, please. Sorry."

"Roj."

It is not really enjoyable to fly like this, for I must always relate that little constellation to the outline of an airplane that I know is there, and fly my own airplane in relation to the mental outline. One light shines on the steel length of a drop tank, and the presence of the drop tank makes it easier to visualize the airplane that I assume is near me in the darkness. If there is one type of flying more difficult than dark-night formation, it is dark-night formation in weather, and the haze thickens at our altitude. I would much rather be on the ground. I would much rather be sitting in a comfortable chair with a pleasant evening sifting by me. But the fact remains that I am sitting in a yellow-handled ejection seat and that before I can feel the comfort of any evening again I must first successfully complete this flight through the night and through whatever weather and difficulties lie ahead. I am not worried, for I have flown many flights in many airplanes, and have not yet damaged an airplane or my desire to fly them.

France Control calls, asking that we change to frequency 355.8. France Control has just introduced me to the face of death. I slide my airplane away from leader's just a little, and divert my attention to turning four separate knobs that will let me listen, on a new frequency, to what they have to say. It takes a moment in the red light to turn the knobs. I look up to see the bright lights of Lead beginning to dim in the haze. I will lose him. Forward on the throttle, catch up with him before he disappears in the mist. Hurry.

Very suddenly in the deceptive mist I am closing too quickly on his wing and his lights are very very bright. Look out, you'll run right into him! He is so helpless as he flies on instruments. He couldn't dodge now if he knew that I would hit him. I slam the throttle back to *idle,* jerk the nose of my airplane up, and roll so that I am upside down, watching the lights of his airplane through the top of my canopy.

Then, very quickly, he is gone. I see my flashlight where it has fallen to the plexiglass over my head, silhouetted by the diffused yellow glow in the low cloud that is a city preparing to sleep on the ground. What an unusual place for a flashlight. I begin the roll to recover to level flight, but I move the stick too quickly, at what has become far too low an airspeed. I am stunned. My airplane is spinning. It snaps around once and the glow is all about me. I look for references, for ground or stars; but there is only the faceless glow. The stick shakes convulsively in my hand and the airplane snaps around again. I do not know whether the airplane is in an erect spin or an inverted spin, I know only that one must never spin a swept-wing aircraft. Not even in broad light and clear day. Instruments. Attitude indicator shows that the spin has stopped, by itself or by my monstrous efforts on the stick and rudder. It shows that the airplane is wings-level inverted; the two little bars of the artificial horizon that always point to the ground are pointing now to the canopy overhead.

I must bail out. I must not stay in an uncontrolled airplane below 10,000 feet. The altimeter is an unwinding blur. I must raise the right armrest, squeeze the trigger, before it is too late.

There is a city beneath me. I promised myself that I would never leave an airplane over a city.

Give it one more chance to recover on instruments, I haven't given the airplane a chance to fly itself out.

The ground must be very close.

There is a strange low roaring in my ears.

Fly the attitude indicator.

Twist the wings level.

Speed brakes out.

I must be very close to the ground, and the ground is not the friend of airplanes that dive into it.

Pull out.

Roaring in my ears. Glow in the cloud around me.

St. Elmo's fire on the windscreen, blue and dancing. The last time I saw St. Elmo's fire was over Albuquerque, last year with Bo Beaven.

Pull out.

Well, I am waiting, death. The ground is very close, for the glow is bright and the roaring is loud. It will come quickly. Will I hear it or will everything just go black? I hold the stick back as hard as I dare—harder would stall the airplane, spin it again.

So this is what dying is like. You find yourself in a situation that has suddenly gone out of control, and you die. And there will be a pile of wreckage and someone will wonder why the pilot didn't eject from his airplane. One must never stay with an uncontrolled airplane below 10,000 feet.

Why do you wait, death? I know I am certain I am convinced that I will hit the ground in a few thousandths of a second. I am tense for the impact. I am not really ready to die, but now that is just too bad. I am shocked and surprised and interested in meeting death. The waiting for the crash is unbearable.

And then I am suddenly alive again.

The airplane is climbing.

I am alive.

The altimeter sweeps through 6,000 feet in a swift rush of a climb. Speed brakes *in*. Full forward with the throttle. I am climbing. Wings level, airspeed a safe 350 knots, the glow is fading below. The accelerometer shows that I pulled seven and a half G's in my recovery from the dive. I didn't feel one of them, even though my G-suit was not plugged into its source of pressured air.

"Red lead, this is Two here; had a little difficulty, climbing back through 10,000 feet . . ."

"TEN THOUSAND FEET?"

"Roger, I'll be up with you in a minute, we can rejoin over Toul TACAN."

Odd. And I was so sure that I would be dead.

The flashes in the dark clouds north of Phalsbourg are more frequent and flicker now from behind my airplane as well as in front of it. They are good indicators of thunderstorm cells, and they do not exactly fit my definition of "scattered." Directly ahead, on course, are three quick

[149]

bright flashes in a row. Correct 30 degrees left. Alone. Time for twisted thoughts in the back of the mind. "You have to be crazy or just plain stupid to fly into a thunderstorm in an eighty-four F." The words are my words, agreed and illustrated by other pilots who had circumstance force them to fly this airplane through an active storm cell.

The airplane, they say, goes almost completely out of control, and despite the soothing words of the flight handbook, the pilot is relying only on his airplane's inertia to hurl it through and into smooth air beyond the storm.

But still I have no intention of penetrating one of the flickering monsters ahead. And I see that my words were wrong. I face the storms on my course now through a chain of logic that any pilot would have followed. The report called them "scattered," not numerous or continuous. I flew on. There are at least four separate radar-equipped facilities below me capable of calling vectors through the worst cells. I fly on. A single-engine pilot does not predicate his action on what-shall-I-do-if-the-radio-goes-out. The risk of the mission is worth the result of delivering the heavy canvas sack in the gun bay.

Now, neither crazy nor stupid, I am at the last link of the chain: I dodge the storms by the swerving radiocompass needle and the flashes of lightning that I see from the cockpit. The TACAN is not in the least disturbed by my uneasy state of mind. The only thing that matters in the world of its transistorized brain is that we are 061 miles from Phalsbourg, slightly to the left of course. The radiocompass has gone wild, pointing left and right and ahead and behind. Its panic is disconcerting among the level-headed coolness of the other instruments, and my right glove moves its function switch to *off*. Gratefully accepting the sedative, the needle slows, and stops.

Flash to the left, alter course 10 degrees right. Flash behind the right wing, forget about it. Flash-FLASH directly brilliantly ahead and the instrument panel goes featureless and white. There is no dodging this one. Scattered.

The storm, in quick sudden hard cold fury, grips my airplane in its jaws and shakes it as a furious terrier shakes a rat. Right glove is tight on the stick. Instrument panel, shock-mounted, slams into blur. The tin horizon whips from an instant 30-degree left bank to an instant 60-degree right bank. That is not possible. A storm is only air.

Left glove, throttle full forward. My airplane, in slow motion, yaws dully to the left. Right rudder, hard. Like a crash landing on a deep-rutted rock trail. Yaw to the right. My airplane has been drugged, she will not respond. Vicious left rudder.

The power, where is the power? Left glove back, forward again, as far as it will go, as hard as it will go. A shimmering blurred line where the tachometer needle should be. Less than 90 percent rpm at full throttle.

I hear the airplane shaking. I cannot hear the engine. Stick and rudders are useless moving pieces of metal. I cannot control my airplane. But throttle, I need the throttle. What is wrong?

Ice. The intake guide vanes are icing, and the engine is not getting air. I see intake clogged in grey ice. Flash and FLASH the bolt is a brilliant snake of incandescent noon-white sun in the dark. I cannot see. Everything has gone red and I cannot even see the blurred panel. I feel the stick I feel the throttle I cannot see. I have suddenly a ship in the sky, and the storm is breaking it. So quickly. This cannot last. Thunderstorms cannot hurt fighters. I am on my way to Chaumont. Important mission.

Slowly, through the bone-jarring shake of the storm, I

can see again. The windscreen is caked with grey ice and bright blue fire. I have never seen the fire so brightly blue. My wings are white. I am heavy with ice and I am falling and the worst part of a thunderstorm is at the lowest altitudes. I cannot take much more of this pounding. White wings, covered in shroud. Right glove grips the stick, for that is what has kept my airplane in the sky for six years. But tonight the airplane is very slow and does not respond, as if she were suddenly very tired and did not care to live. As if her engine had been shut down.

The storm is a wild horse of the desert that has suddenly discovered a monster on its back. It is in a frenzy to rid itself of me, and it strikes with shocks so fast they cannot be seen. I learn a new fact. The ejection seat is not always an escape. Bailout into the storm will be just as fatal as the meeting of earth and airplane, for in the churning air my parachute would be a tangled nylon rag. My airplane and I have been together for a long time, we will stay together now. The decision bolts the ejection seat to the cockpit floor, the *Thunderstreak* and I smash down through the jagged sky as a single dying soul. My arm is heavy on the stick, and tired. It will be good to rest. There is a roaring in my ears, and I feel the hard ground widening about me, falling up to me.

So this is the way it will end. With a violent shuddering of airplane and an unreadable instrument panel; with a smothered engine and heavy white wings. Again the feeling: I am not really ready to end the game. I have told myself that this day would come to meet me, as inevitably as the ground which rushes to meet me now, and yet I think, quickly, of a future lost. It cannot be helped. I am falling through a hard splintering storm with a control stick that is not a control stick. I am a chip in a hurricane a raindrop in a typhoon about to become one with the sea a mass of pieces-to-be a concern of air traffic controllers and air police and gendarmerie and coroners and accident investigators and statisticians and newspaper reporters and a board of officers and a theater commander and a wing commander and a squadron commander and a little circle of friends. I am a knight smashed from his square and thrown to the side of the chessboard.

Tomorrow morning there will be no storm and the sun will be shining on the quiet bits of metal that used to be Air Force Jet Two Niner Four Zero Five.

But at this instant there is a great heavy steel-bladed storm that is battering and crushing me down, out of the sky, and the thing that follows this instant is another just like it.

Altimeter is a blur, airspeed is a blur, vertical speed is a blur, attitude indicator is a quick-rocking blurred luminous line that does not respond to my orders. Any second now, as before, I am tense and waiting. There will be an impact, and blackness and quiet. Far in the back of my mind, behind the calm fear, is curiosity and a patient waiting. And a pride. I am a pilot. I would be a pilot again.

The terrier flings the rat free.

The air is instantly smooth, and soft as layered smoke. Altimeter three thousand feet airspeed one-ninety knots vertical speed four thousand feet per minute down attitude indicator steep right bank heading indicator one seven zero degrees tachometer eighty-three percent rpm at full throttle. Level the white wings. Air is warm. Thudthudthud from the engine as ice tears from guide vanes and splinters into compressor blades. Wide slabs of ice rip from the wings. Half the windscreen is suddenly clear. Faint blue fire on the glass. Power is taking hold: 90 percent on the tachometer

... thud ... 91 percent ... thudthud ... 96 percent. Airspeed coming up through 240 knots, left turn, climb. Five hundred feet per minute, 700 feet per minute altimeter showing 3,000 feet and climbing I am 50 degrees off course and I don't care attitude indicator showing steady left climbing turn I'm alive the oil pressure is good utility and power hydraulic pressure are good I don't believe it voltmeter and loadmeter showing normal control stick is smooth and steady how strange it is to be alive windscreen is clear thud 99 percent rpm tailpipe temperature is in the green. Flash-FLASH look out to the left look out! Hard turn right I'll never make it through another storm tonight forget the flight plan go north of Phalsbourg 15,000 feet 320 knots flash to the left and behind, faint.

And strangely, the words of an old pilot's song: ". . . for I, am, too young, to die . . ." It is a good feeling, this being alive. Something I haven't appreciated. I have learned again.

Rpm is up to 100 percent. I am climbing, and 20,000 feet is below flash 21,000 feet is below. Blue fire washes across the windscreen as if it did not know that a windscreen is just a collection of broken bits of glass.

What a ridiculous thought. A windscreen is a windscreen, a solid piece of six-ply plate glass, for keeping out the wind and the rain and the ice and a place to look through and a place to shine the gunsight. I will be looking through windscreens for a long time to come.

Why didn't I bail out? Because the seat was bolted to the cockpit floor. No. Because I decided not to bail out into the storm. I should have bailed out. I definitely should have left the airplane. Better to take my chances with a rough descent in a torn chute than certain death in a crash. I should have dropped the external tanks, at least. Would have made the airplane lighter and easier to control. Now, at 32,000 feet, I think of dropping the tanks. Quick thinking.

Flash.

I flew out of the storm, and that is what I wanted to do. I am glad now that I did not drop the tanks; there would have been reports to write and reasons to give. When I walk away from my airplane tonight I will have only one comment to make on the Form One: UHF transmitter and receiver failed during flight. I will be the only person to know that the United States Air Force in Europe came within a few seconds of losing an airplane.

Flashflash. Ahead.

I have had enough storm-flying for one night. Throttle to 100 percent and climb. I will fly over the weather for the rest of the way home; there will be one cog slipping tonight in the European Air Traffic Control System, above the weather near Phalsbourg. The cog has earned it.

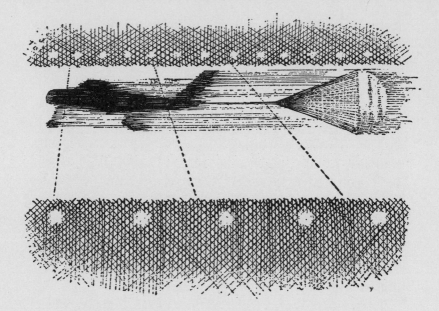

CHAPTER SIX

The people on the ground who operate the air traffic control system are very important people, but not indispensable. The system, although it is a good one, is not an indispensable system. Airplanes were flying long before the first sign of air traffic control appeared, they will go on flying if it all suddenly disappears.

When the rules of the air were set down, there was a very wise man present who knew that cogs will slip now and then, and that the system had best be flexible. I am still in command of my airplane, and I will put it where I think that it is best for it to go, system or no system. Now I have decided that I would rather not engage another thunderstorm. I climb away from my assigned altitude of 33,000 feet to seek the clear air and smooth flying above the clouds. I am passing through altitudes that might have been assigned to other airplanes, and there is the possibility of midair collision.

Yet the chance of my colliding with another airplane is almost nonexistent. I am off course; in order to collide with me, another airplane would have to be precisely as far off course as I am.

Though I have not talked to a ground station for a long while, I have not been forgotten; I am a flight plan written on a strip of paper at all the stations along my route. Other airplanes will be told of my course and my estimated times over those stations.

I am a quarter-inch dot on the radar screens, and controllers will vector other airplanes around me.

The primary reason that I will not collide with any other airplane is that my *Thunderstreak* is 43 feet 3 inches long, its wingspan is 33 feet 6 inches, and it flies in a block of air that is a thousand cubic miles of empty space. And so I climb.

My approach time to Chaumont will be held open for a half hour past my estimated time of arrival. I dial the familiar channel 55 on the TACAN and listen to the identifier. Chaumont. I never would have thought that a little French village could be so like Home. Bearing is 239 degrees, distance is 093 miles. Phalsbourg is drifting behind me to the left. I should have reported over the French border and over Phalsbourg. But the cog is slipping.

Thirty-eight thousand feet on the altimeter and still no top to the cloud. The blue fire is gone. Fuel is down to 2,700 pounds, and at this weight a practical ceiling for my plane will be about 43,000 feet. It is rare to have clouds in

[157]

Europe that top at more than 40,000 feet, and I am not concerned. My interest is directed only over the instruments in front of me. There is now, without a radio, no other world.

The old pilots tell of days when it was "needle-ball and alcohol" through the weather: a turn-and-bank indicator and a magnetic compass their only aid in the cloud. But this is a modern age, and tonight I fly by the seven instruments in the center of the panel, and have my navigation solved second by second in the two dials of the TACAN.

If the inverter that changes the generator's DC power to AC were to fail, my gyro instruments, attitude indicator and heading indicator would slowly run down into uselessness. But the '84F is an American airplane, and therefore has safety systems for the safety systems. In this instance, the safety factor is called the alternate instrument inverter, waiting to drive the gyros should the engine-driven generator or the main inverter fail. Should both inverters fail, I am moved back through the years to fly a fighter airplane by needle-ball and alcohol.

There is a light tremble through my airplane as I climb through 40,000 feet, and the wings begin to rock. There has been no lightning. I scan the windscreen, looking for ice. I cannot carry much ice and continue to climb. The windscreen is clear.

With no sound and with no warning, like the magician's silk from above the hawk, the cloud is gone. In one instant I am checking for ice, in the next I am looking through the glass, as through a narrow gothic arch in steel, at two hundred miles of crystal air, floored 20,000 feet below by unruffled cloud. It is vertigo, as if I had run over a hidden cliff and discovered myself in thin air. Right glove tightens on the stick.

I have flown from a sheer wall of cloud, and it tumbles away toward the earth like the mountains south of Strasbourg tumble away to the valley of the Rhine. The giant wall swings in wide arc to my left and right, and it flickers here and there with its storms.

I am an invisible speck of dust sifting on a tiny breath of air.

A hundred and fifty miles behind me to the north, the wall becomes the smooth gentle-rising slope that I entered long ago. But this is helpless knowledge, for I can see in the starlight that the only real thing in all the world is the awesome mass of cloud around my 43-foot airplane. There is no ground, there is no steady glow of lighted city through the floor of the mist. There is not one other flashing navigation light from horizon to horizon. I am alone, with one thousand stars for company.

I rest my helmet against the ejection seat headrest and look out again at the sky. The sky is not blue or purple or merely black. It is a deep meadow of powdered carbon, a bed for the stars. Around me.

Back with the throttle, to make the engine quiet. Right glove reaches to the three knobs that control the red light of the cockpit, and my own little red world fades into the meadow.

The dust mote settles gently back toward 33,000 feet, and its voice is the barest whisper in the dimension of the night.

I am one man. Tonight, perhaps, I am Man, alive and looking out over my planet toward my galaxy, crystallizing in myself, for a span of seconds, the centuries of looking out from this little earth that Man has done.

We have much in common, we men.

Tonight I, who love my airplane with all its moods and

hardships and joys, am looking out upon the stars. And to-night, 20 minutes to the east, there is another pilot, another man who loves his airplane, looking out at these same stars. These symbols.

My airplane is painted with a white star, his with a red star. It is dark, and paint is hard to see. In his cockpit is the same family of flight instruments and engine instruments and radio control panels that is in my cockpit. In his airplane as in mine, when the stick is pressed to the left, the airplane banks to the left.

I know, unquestioningly, that I would like the man in that cockpit. We could talk through the long night of the airplanes that we have known and the times that we were afraid and the places that we have been. We would laugh over the half-witted things that we did when we were new in the air. We have shared many things, he and I, too many things to be ordered into our airplanes to kill each other.

I went through flying training at a base near Dallas, he went through it at a base near Stalingrad. My flight instructors shouted at me in English, his at him in Russian. But the blue fire trickles once in a while across his windscreen as it does across mine, and ice builds and breaks over his wings as it does mine. And somewhere in his cockpit is a control panel or a circuit breaker panel or a single switch that he has almost to stand on his head to reach. Perhaps at this moment his daughter is considering whether or not to accept a pair of Siamese kittens. Look out for your curtains, friend.

I wish that I could warn him about the kittens.

Fifty miles from Chaumont. Fifty miles and Through the Looking-Glass of cloud and rain and Hi there, ace, how'd the crosscountry go? Fifty miles is a very long way.

I have a not-working radio, above the clouds. Not a

great problem, but enough of one so that I force my attention from the peaceful meadow of black to the task of putting my airplane back on the earth. Throttle forward at 33,000 feet, and again the rumble and whines and squeaks and moans from my comic in spinning steel.

No radio. I can fly on to the west, looking for a hole in the clouds, descend, fly back to Chaumont and land. A very poor plan for the fuel that remains in my tanks and for the vagaries of French weather.

I can fly a triangular pattern to the left, with one-minute legs. After a few patterns, a radar site will notice my path and its direction, vector an interceptor to me, and I will fly a letdown and instrument approach as his wingman. A drastic plan, but one to remember as a last-ditch, last-resort action.

I can fly a letdown at Chaumont as I had planned, hoping that the weather is not so bad that I need a Ground Controlled Approach in order to find the runway. At last report the weather was not so bad. If I do not break out of the weather at the TACAN low-approach minimum altitude, I will climb back on top and try a penetration at my alternate, Etain Air Base, ten minutes to the north. I have just enough fuel for this plan, and I shall follow it. For interest's sake, I will try my radio once more when I am directly over Chaumont. One can never tell about UHF radios.

Forty miles. Five minutes. To home. But months still to a home where there is a wife and daughter and where the people in the towns speak English.

The bulletin board in the Chaumont pilots' quarters is a mass of newspaper clippings from that older Home. On the board are charges and countercharges concerning the wisdom of recalling the Guard without a war to make it necessary. There are letters to the editors from wives and families and employers, asking questions and offering answers. The newspapers tell of poor conditions into which we were forced, of our trials and our difficulties, of the state of our morale. The picture they paint is a bleak one, but our lot is not really so bleak.

I left an interesting civilian job, flying small airplanes and writing for an aviation magazine, and was ordered back into the Air Force. It was disrupting, of course. But then I have never before been needed by the country to which I owe so much. I would be happier in the freedom of my old life, but my country has come fearfully close to war. The recall was not convenient for me or for my family, but it was a wise plan of action. The recall showed that Air Guard pilots were not merely sportsmen at government expense; a feeling that I sometimes harbored, guiltily, after pleasant weekends spent flying military airplanes, at $80 per weekend.

My squadron crossed the Atlantic in three hops. It made the crossing without air refueling, without proper air navigation stations covering the route, without an incident. We landed at Chaumont Air Base one month after we were called to active duty, flying whenever ceilings were higher than 500 feet.

The multiengine pilots in their tremendous airplanes brought hundreds of tons of support equipment and parts and supplies. We listened to briefings from NATO pilots about the strange new world of European air traffic control. Ammunition specialists emptied boxcars of 50-caliber machinegun bullets and racks of olive-drab, yellow-striped high-explosive bombs and long aluminum tanks of napalm and rack on rack of slim unpainted rockets. We were assigned areas of battle and we met with the army that we were to support. We held practice alerts that began as chaos, progressed through orderly confusion, and became, finally, quick and efficient.

Though the complaints are made and duly printed, though the crisis that called us has subsided, we accomplished the task set for us. We arrived in France with all our pilots and all our airplanes. Today the Alert pilots play bridge and chess and pingpong near the red telephone.

Not all without cost, of course. To date, our readiness has cost Don Slack, pilot, and the flags are still at half-mast.

For us who fly the '84F, the mobilization is one long weekend of Air Guard duty. In town the people speak a different language, and there are sentries and rolls of barbed wire surrounding the flight line, but we fly with the same friends (except one) and the same airplanes (except one) that we have always flown with, and the life is not cause for complaint (except one). We fly, and the sky of France is much the same as the sky of home. Wind and rain and sun and stars. It is its own kind of home, the sky, and for the brief hours of my flight I do not miss the other home across the sea. I do miss Don Slack.

The stars glow steadily in the darkness of their meadow, part of my world. I think, for a moment, of all that has been said of the enchantment of this cathedral of air. A million words, written and spoken and turned to photograph, in which people who fly risk the curse of sentiment, that deadly curse, to tell of what they have seen. The enchantment does not lend itself to paper and ink or to syllables, or even to sensitized film, but the people's risk of the curse is itself witness to the sight and the mood that awaits the man who travels the high land. Cloud and star and bow

[163]

of color are just so many words to be laid carefully in a shallow grave of corrasable bond. The sky, in the end, can only be called an interesting place. My beloved sky.

The wide needle of the TACAN wobbles, the distance-measuring drum turns through 006, and it is time to put my set of plans into action.

I begin the left turn into the holding pattern, and my right glove half-turns the cockpit light rheostats, soaking itself in soft red. The IFF dial goes to Mode Three, Code 70. I should now be an identified and expected dot on the radar screen of Chaumont Radar. Thumb down very hard on microphone button, throttle back, speed brakes out and the rumble of shattering air as they extend from the sides of the plane. "Chaumont Approach Control, Jet Four Zero Five, high station on the TACAN, requesting latest Chaumont weather." There is a sidetone. A good sign. But there is no reply.

Fly along the pattern, recheck defrosters and pitot heat *on,* a quick review of the penetration: heading 047 degrees outbound from the holding pattern, left descending turn to heading 197 degrees, level at 3,500 feet and in to the 12-mile gate.

I level now at 20,000 feet, power at 85 percent rpm and ready in my mind for the letdown.

". . . measured nine hundred feet overcast, visibility five miles in light rain, altimeter two niner eight five."

I have never had a more capricious radio. Hard down on the plastic button. "Chaumont Approach, Zero Five leaving flight level Two Zero Zero present time, requesting GCA frequency." Stick forward, nose down, and I am through 19,000 feet, through 18,000 feet, through 17,000 feet, with airspeed smooth at 350 knots.

". . . ive, your radar frequency will be three four four point six, local channel one five."

"Roj, Approach, leaving your frequency." In the left bank of the turn, I click the channel selector to one five. And back to the instruments. Look out for vertigo. "He went into the weather in a bank, and he came out of it upside down." But not me and not tonight; I have come through worse than vertigo, and I have been warned. "Chaumont Radar, Jet Four Zero Five, how do you read on three four four point six." A pause, and time to doubt the errant radio.

"Read you five square, Zero Five, how do you read Radar?" So the radio becomes better as I descend. Interesting.

"Five by."

"Roger, Zero Five, we have you in positive radar contact one eight miles north of Chaumont. Continue your left turn to heading one three five degrees, level at two thousand five hundred feet. This will be a precision approach to runway one niner; length eight thousand fifty feet, width one hundred fifty feet, touchdown elevation one thousand seventy five feet. If you lose communication with Radar for any one minute in the pattern or any thirty seconds on final approach . . ."

I am gratefully absorbed in familiar detail. Continue the turn, let the nose down a little more to speed the descent, recheck engine screens retracted and pneumatic compressor *off* and oxygen 100 percent and engine instruments in the green and hook again the lanyard to the D-ring of the parachute ripcord. My little world rushes obediently down as I direct it. Concentrating on my instruments, I do not notice when I again enter the cloud.

The voice continues, directing me through the black with

[165]

the assurance of a voice that has done this many times. The man behind the voice is an enlisted man, to whom I speak only on official business. But now I give myself and my airplane wholly to his voice and rank is a pompous thing. Microphone button down.

"Zero Five is level . . ." No sidetone. I am not transmitting. Microphone button down hard and rocking in its little mount under the left thumb. "Zero Five is level, two thousand five hundred feet, steady one three five degrees." Flaps down. Airspeed slows through 220 knots. Left glove on the clear plastic wheel-shaped handle of the landing gear lever. A mechanical movement: pull the handle out a quarter-inch and push it down six inches. At the instant that the lever slams down into its slot, the tall hard wheels of my airplane break from their hidden wells and press down, shuddering, into the rush of cloud. Three bright green lights flare at the left of the instrument panel. Speed brake switch forward.

"Zero Five has three green, pressure and brakes." Tap the brakes.

"Roger, Zero Five, you are now one zero miles from touchdown, recheck your gear, the tower has cleared you for a full-stop landing. Turn heading one seven five, stand by this frequency for final controller." Inside the rain-spattered red-checkered Ground Control Approach van at the side of Chaumont's only runway, the search controller looks across to his companion, framed dimly in the green light of his own radar screen. "He's all yours, Tommy." Tommy nods.

"Jet Zero Five, this is your final controller, how do you read?" He already knows that I can hear him very well. The procedure is part of a time-honored ritual.

"Zero Five reads you five by." And I say with him to

myself his next words, the lines assigned to him in the script for his role as GCA Final Approach Controller.

"Roger, Zero Five," we say. "You need not acknowledge any further transmissions, however there will be periodic transmission breaks on final approach which will be identified." Fuel aboard shows just under 2,000 pounds on the big tank gage. At my airplane's present weight, I should fly down final approach at 165 knots. "Repeat the tower has cleared you for a full-stop . . ."

When I am under the direction of a good GCA operator, I might just as well be on the ramp and shutting down my engine, for my landing is absolutely certain.

". . . you are thirty seconds from the glide path, correcting left to right on the centerline. Turn heading one eight zero. One eight zero. Transmission break." He lifts his foot from the microphone pedal on the floor under his screen, giving me a few seconds to speak. I have nothing to say to fill his silence, and his foot comes down again. "One eight zero is bringing you out on centerline, drifting slightly from left to right. Ten seconds to glide path. Turn one seven niner. One seven niner . . ." That is a little compliment for me. One-degree corrections are very small, very precise, and require smooth aircraft control from the pilot. I hear one-degree corrections only in still air, only when I am flying well. A smile under the oxygen mask. He should have seen me thirty minutes ago.

"On glide path, begin descent. Suggest an initial rate of descent of seven hundred fifty feet per minute for your aircraft . . ." What could be simpler than flying a GCA through the weather to the runway? There are the cross-barred pointers of the Instrument Landing System to accomplish the same job, but the ILS is not human. Technically, an ILS approach is more consistently accurate than a GCA, but I would much rather work with a good man behind a good radar, in any weather. Speed brakes out with left thumb aft on sawtooth switch. I lower the nose, visualizing as I do the long slide of the invisible glide slope in front of me. The rate of climb needle points on the *down* side of its scale to 1,000 feet per minute, then moves back to 800 feet per minute.

"Rolled out nicely on glide path . . . on centerline . . . drifting now slightly left of centerline, turn heading one eight three degrees, one eight three. On glide path . . ." Airspeed is 170 knots, back on the throttle for a second, then up again. Airspeed 168. Back again and up again. 165.

"Going five feet low on glide path, adjust your rate of descent slightly . . . on centerline . . . transmission break." I think the stick back a little, think it very slightly forward again.

"Up and on glide path, resume normal rate of descent. On centerline . . . on glide path . . . on centerline . . . an excellent rate of descent . . ." Sometimes, I would bet, a GCA operator runs out of things to say. But he is required to give continuous direction to aircraft on final approach. What a boring life he must lead. But bored or not, I am very glad to hear him.

"On glide path . . . doing a nice job of it, lieutenant . . . on centerline . . . tower reports breaking action good . . ." How does he know that I am a lieutenant? I could be a major or a colonel out in the night weather to check on the standardization of GCA operators. But I am not, I am just a man happy to be through a storm and grateful to hear again a voice on my long-silent radio.

". . . you are two miles from touchdown, on glide path, going ten feet left of centerline, turn right heading one eight four degrees . . . one eight four. On glide path correcting back to centerline . . . one eight four . . . a mile and a half from touchdown . . ."

I look up, and realize suddenly that I have been out of the cloud for seconds. The red and green and twin white rows of runway lights stretch directly ahead. Back a fraction on the throttle, slowing down.

". . . one mile from touchdown, going ten feet low on the glide path . . ." Here it comes. I know it, the final controller knows it. I drop below the glide path when I have the runway in sight. If I were to stay completely under his direction, I would touch down some 600 feet down the runway, and that is 600 feet I can well use. It takes normal landing distance and 2,000 feet more to stop my airplane if the drag chute fails on a wet runway. And regardless of drag chute, regardless of airplane, I learned as a cadet to recite the three most useless things to a pilot: Runway behind you, altitude above you, and a tenth of a second ago.

Though I listen offhandedly to the GCA operator's voice, I fly now by only one instrument: the runway. Landing lights on. Left glove reaches ahead and touches a switch down to make two powerful columns of white light pivot from beneath my wings, turning forward to make a bright path in the droplets of rain.

". . . one quarter mile from touchdown, you are going thirty feet below the glide path, bring your aircraft up . . ." I wish that he would be quiet now. I need his voice in the weather, but I do not need him to tell me how to land my airplane when I can see the runway. The columns of light are speeding over white concrete now, redlights, greenlights flash below.

". . . thirty-five feet below glide path, you are too low for a safe approach, bring your aircraft up . . ."

Quiet, GCA. You should have more sense than to go to

pieces when I begin the flareout. Either I am happy with a touchdown on the first few hundred feet of runway or you are happy with my airplane landing 600 feet along a wet runway. Stick back, throttle to *idle,* stick back, a bit of left aileron . . . I feel for the runway with my sensitive wheels. Down another foot, another few inches. Come on, runway.

Hard rubber on hard concrete. Not as smooth a touchdown as I wanted but not bad   stick forward let the nosewheel down   squeak of 14-inch wheel taking its share of 19,000 pounds of airplane   right glove on yellow drag chute handle and a quick short pull. Glove waits on handle ready to jettison the chute if it weathervanes and pulls me suddenly toward the edge of the runway. I am thrown gently forward in my shoulder harness by the silent pouf of a 16-foot ring-slot parachute billowing from the tail. Speed brakes in, flaps up, boots carefully off the brakes. The drag chute will stop me almost before I am ready to stop. I must turn off the runway before I may jettison the chute; if I stop too soon and have to taxi to the turnoff with this great blossom of nylon behind me, I would need almost full power to move at more than two miles per hour. It is an effective drag chute.

We roll smoothly to the end of the runway, and even without braking I must add a burst of throttle to turn off at the end. Boot on left pedal and we turn. Drag chute handle twisted and pulled again, as I look back over my shoulder. The white blossom is suddenly gone and my airplane rolls more easily along the taxiway.

Left glove pulls the canopy lock handle aft, right glove grips the frame and swings the roof of my little world up and out of the way, overhead. Rain pelts lightly on my face above the green rubber mask. It is cool rain, and familiar, and I am glad to feel it. Landing lights *off and retracted* taxi light *on,* ejection seat safety pin from the G-suit pocket and into its hold in the armrest, UHF radio to tower frequency.

"Chaumont Tower, Jet Four Zero Five is clear the active runway, taxi to the squadron hangar."

"Cleared taxi via the parallel taxiway, Zero Five. We had no late estimate on your time of arrival at Chaumont. Did you have difficulties enroute?"

Tower feels chatty this evening. "A little radio trouble, tower."

"Read you five square now, Zero Five."

"Roj."

Right glove presses the shiny fastener at the side of my mask as I glide between the rows of blue taxiway lights, pushed by the soft sigh of engine at 50 percent rpm. Cool rain on my face. We trundle together in a right turn, my airplane and I, up a gentle hill, and follow after the green letters of a Follow Me truck that appears suddenly out of the darkness.

Above this dark rain and above the clouds of its birth is a world that belongs only to pilots. Tonight it belonged, for a moment, only to me and to my airplane, and across the breadth of it to the east, to another pilot and another airplane. We shared the sky tonight, and perhaps even now he is tasting the cool raindrops as he taxies by a runway that is as much a target in my intelligence folders as Chaumont Air Base is a target in his.

And I understand, in the rain, that although tonight there has been only he and I in our airplanes, tomorrow it will be some other one of Us and some other one of Them. When my little scene is played and I am once again back in the United States and a pilot of the New Jersey Air National Guard, there will still be someone flying the

European night in a white-starred airplane and one in a red-starred one. Only the faces in the cockpits change.

Share work, share dedication, share danger, share triumph, share fear, share joy, share love, and you forge a bond that is not subject to change. I'll leave Europe for America, He'll leave Europe for Russia. The faces change, the bond is always there.

Hard on the right brake, swing around into the concrete pad of a parking revetment, nose pointing out toward the taxiway and the runway beyond. Taxi light *off*, check that the ground crew from the Follow Me truck slide the chocks in front of the tall wheels.

May you have the sense and the guidance to stay out of thunderstorms, distant friend.

Throttle back swiftly to *off*. The faithful spinning buffoon in steel dies with a long fading airy sigh, pressing the last of its heat, a shimmering black wave, into the night. Sleep well.

A slap on the side of the fuselage. "Run-down!" the crew chief calls, and I check my watch. It took 61 seconds for the turbine and the compressor to stop their sigh. Important information, for a maintenance man, and I enter the time in the Form One.

Inverter *off*, fuel *off*, UHF radio *off*, and at last, battery *off*. There is one last heavy click in the night as the battery switch goes to *off* under my glove, and my airplane is utterly and completely still.

In the beam of my issue flashlight, I write in the form that the UHF radio transmitter and receiver operate erratically above 20,000 feet. There is no space in which to enter the fact that the Air Force is lucky to have this airplane back at all. I log 45 minutes of night weather, one hour of night, one TACAN penetration, one GCA, one drag chute landing. I sign the form, unsnap the safety belt and shoulder harness and survival kit and G-suit and oxygen hose and microphone cable and soft chinstrap.

A blue Air Force station wagon arrives, splashing light on my nosewheel, and the sack from above the guns is handed down.

I lay my white helmet on the canopy bow in front of me and climb stiffly down the yellow ladder from the lonely little world that I love. I sign a paper, the station wagon leaves me in the dark. Helmet in hand, scarf pressed again by the wind, I am back on the ground of my air base in France, with a thousand other civilians in uniform, and with 31 . . . no, with 30 . . . other pilots.

My airplane is quiet, and for a moment still an alien, still a stranger to the ground, I am home.

AIRCRAFT TYPE AND NO.			PILOT		FROM			TO	
F-84F 29405			BACH		WETHERSFIELD			CHAUMONT	

ALTERNATE				TOTAL DISTANCE	TAKE-OFF TIME			TOTAL AMT FUEL	
ETAIN				573	2130			7400 #	

ROUTE (Check points)	NAV	IDENT FREQ	RPT	IDENT FREQ	MAG HEAD	LEG REMAIN	ETE	EST TOTAL	ETA ATA	GROUND SPEED	EST LEG REMAIN	ACTUAL FUEL REMAIN
CLIMB FL 330	SOPLEY RADAR 339.1		ANGLIA CONTROL		165							
ABBEVILLE	AB 387				165	123 450	30	30			2600 4800	
LAON	LC 77		LC 344		120	72 378	9	39		465 TAS	440 4360	
FRANCE/ GERMANY	RHEIN CONTROL 341.4				084	50 328	7	46			350 4010	
SPANGDAHLEM	SPA 100		SPA 428		084	75 253	10	56			470 3540	
WIESBADEN	WAB 34				093	65 188	9	1+05			440 3100	
GERMANY/ FRANCE					093	67 121	9	1+14			440 2660	
PHALSBOURG	PL 102		PL 486		210	26 95	3	1+17			140 2520	
CHAUMONT	CU 55		CU 515		249	95 0	12	1+29			550 1970	
ETAIN	ER 99				040	60	8				390 1580	

POSITION REPORT

IDENT	POSITION	TIME	ALT	IFR (VFR)	EST NEXT FIX	NAME OF SUCCEEDING REPTG PT

GLOSSARY OF TERMS USED IN THIS BOOK

Accelerometer—An instrument that measures the number of G units to which an aircraft is subjected, in multiples of normal gravity, or one G.

Ailerons—Surfaces near the wingtips which are actuated by the control stick to bank the aircraft left or right or to roll it completely about its longitudinal axis.

Airspeed indicator—An instrument that measures the airplane's speed through the air in nautical miles per hour (knots).

Altimeter—A three-handed pressure instrument that reads aircraft height above sea level.

ATO—Assisted TakeOff. For short ground rolls during takeoff, up to four jettisonable rocket engines can be attached to the fuselage of the F-84F. Each engine fires for 14 seconds and each contributes 1,000 pounds of thrust.

Attitude indicator—Also called "artificial horizon" or "gyro horizon." An instrument containing a gyro-stabilized face that remains parallel to the true horizon and a miniature aircraft duplicating the motions and attitude of the true aircraft.

Base leg—In a landing or gunnery pattern, the path of flight followed just before turning to the final or firing approach. On base leg the runway or the target is at right angles to the aircraft heading.

Battle damage switches—A row of four fuel shutoff switches in the F-84F. They prevent the transfer of fuel from other tanks into a fuel tank damaged in combat.

BOQ—Bachelor's Officers' Quarters; the living area of the squadron pilots.

Circuit breaker—A safety switch that acts as an electrical fuse to cut off the flow of current to an overloaded circuit.

COC—Combat Operations Center. The center of a tactical base's co-ordination; the control point from which the wing commander directs operations during combat.

Command radio—The ultra high frequency (UHF) radio transmitter and receiver used for air-to-ground voice communication.

Cuban eight—An aerobatic maneuver consisting of interconnected half-loops and rolls.

D-ring lanyard—A metal snap and nylon lanyard that attaches to the parachute ripcord handle to quickly and automatically open the pilot's parachute in the event of a low-altitude ejection.

[175]

Defensive split—In air combat, an extreme maneuver separating wingman from leader in an attempt to force an attacker into an unfavorable position.

Depression—An angle through which the gunsight image is lowered to adjust for the various trajectories of bombs and rockets. No depression angle is required for machinegun fire.

Drag chute—A strong nylon parachute packed and installed at the tail of the F-84F. When he pulls the drag chute handle in the cockpit, the pilot hopes that the parachute will deploy to slow his airplane during its landing roll.

Drop tanks—Fuel tanks fastened beneath the wing to extend the range of an aircraft. They can be jettisoned in flight to lighten the airplane for combat.

Echelon—A formation of aircraft arranged in a line at an angle to their line of flight.

Engine screens—Retractable steel screens inside the engine air intake at the nose of the airplane to prevent foreign objects from entering the engine and damaging it.

External stores—Any load mounted on the under-wing attachment fittings; bombs, rockets, drop tanks or nuclear weapons.

Flak—Originally, bursts of antiaircraft fire from special-design ground weapons. More loosely used by fighter-bomber pilots, flak includes pistol and rifle fire, sticks, stones, rocks and whatever else the enemy throws in front of an airplane in the hope of bringing it down.

Flaps—Aerodynamic panels mounted in the wing that can be extended for low-speed flight.

Flight level—A form of altitude designation in which, for instance, 33,000 feet becomes "flight level 330."

Fuselage—The "body" of an airplane, to which are attached the wings and tail.

Go-No-Go Speed—A computed speed that is used to determine that an aircraft is accelerating properly during its takeoff roll. If the go-no-go speed is not reached by a selected distance along the runway, takeoff is discontinued.

G-suit—Properly, "anti-G suit." A set of tightly laced inflatable nylon/rubber "chaps" that fill with air during high-G turns and pullouts to keep the pilot's blood from pooling in his legs and consequent blackout or momentary loss of vision.

Gun heater—A unit that keeps the machine guns warm and in firing condition when flying through the cold of high altitudes.

Holding pattern—In instrument flying, a racetrack-shaped pattern around which an airplane flies while waiting for clearance to descend.

IFF—Identification Friend or Foe. An electronic beacon installed in the aircraft that presents a distinctive pattern on a ground radar screen. IFF gives air traffic controllers positive identification of friendly aircraft.

Inverter—An electrical device that converts DC power into AC power for instrument operation. The F-84F has a main and an alternate inverter.

LABS—Low Altitude Bombing System. One method of delivering nuclear weapons.

Loadmeter—An instrument that measures the percentage of electrical generator output being used by all aircraft systems combined.

Machmeter—An indicator that compares the speed of the airplane to the speed of sound. Mach 1 is the speed of sound; maximum speed of the F-84F is about Mach 1.18.

Ordnance—Any form of firepower that can be delivered from an aircraft to a target.

Penetration—A pattern of instrument descent which brings an aircraft from high altitude to a position over the runway ready for landing.

Pipper—The center dot of light in an optical gunsight that shows the converging point of bullets, and the impact points of bombs and rockets.

Pitot system—The aircraft sensing system that measures static and dynamic air pressures for use in the altimeter, airspeed, and vertical speed indicators.

Pneumatic compressor—A compressor installed in the fuselage that recharges the cylinder of high-pressure air used for engine starting.

Radiocompass—A radio connected to an indicator which very often points to selected low-frequency broadcast and navigation stations on the ground.

Radome—The fiberglass housing that covers radar antennas on the nose of multiengine and all-weather air defense airplanes.

Ramp—An area on which airplanes are parked.

Rpm—Revolutions per minute, measured from zero to 100 percent of possible engine speed on a tachometer installed in the cockpit.

Scissors—In air combat, a series of hard turn reversals.

Servomotor—An electric motor, controlled from the cockpit, assisting in the job of aircraft control.

Shoulderboards—Insignia distinguishing cadets from officers and enlisted men in the Air Force.

Sight caging lever—A handle beneath the gunsight that locks the

[177]

delicate working parts of the sight against the shocks of taxiing, takeoff and landing.

Slipstream—The flow of air along the structure of an aircraft in flight.

Spar—The primary component of a wing or tail assembly, upon which most of the structure's loads are taken.

Speed brakes—A pair of large perforated steel slabs on the fuselage aft of the wing. They are hydraulically forced into the slipstream to slow the aircraft quickly from high speeds.

Stabilator—A contraction of "stabilizer" and "elevator"; the one-piece horizontal tail of an F-84F. It is connected to the pilot's control stick and establishes the nose-up/nose-down attitude of the airplane.

TACAN—Tactical Air Navigation. Like the radiocompass, a navigation radio connected to a needle that points to a selected station on the ground. Unlike the radiocompass, it is connected also to Distance Measuring Equipment (DME) that shows the distance in nautical miles from the aircraft to the station.

Thermocouples—A set of temperature sensing probes installed in the exhaust of a jet engine.

Throttle—A lever on the left side of the cockpit through which the pilot controls fuel flow and engine power.

Trim button—A five-position thumb button set at the top of the control stick grip. With the trim button the pilot can adjust the flight control system to allow the lightest "stick forces" during flight.

Turbine blade—Also "turbine bucket." A curved, high-strength steel blade attached to the turbine wheel and mounted in such a way as to catch the fire of the combustion chambers and rotate the wheel.

UHF—In radio communications, ultra high frequency.

Vertical speed indicator—An instrument that measures rates of climb and descent in feet per minute; from zero during level flight to 6,000 fpm when climbing or diving.

Vertigo—Confusion of a pilot's instinctive sense of direction when flying with reference to instruments alone.

Yaw—Motion of an aircraft to the left and right about its vertical axis.

Yo-yo—In air combat, a steep climb and dive exchanging airspeed for altitude in an attempt to gain a more favorable attacking position.

72 73 10 9 8 7 6 5 4 3 2